TILL THE
EXTINCTION
OF THIS
REBELLION

ALSO BY ERIC STERNER

Anatomy of a Massacre: The Destruction of Gnadenhutten, 1782
The Battle of Upper Sandusky, 1782

TILL THE EXTINCTION *OF THIS* REBELLION

George Rogers Clark, Frontier Warfare,
and the Illinois Campaign *of*
1778–1779

ERIC STERNER

WESTHOLME
Yardley

Westholme Publishing, LLC
904 Edgewood Road
Yardley, Pennsylvania 19067
Visit our Web site at www.westholmepublishing.com

ISBN: 978-1-59416-425-5
Also available as an eBook.

Printed in the United States of America.

Contents

Illustrations

MAPS

A gallery of illustrations follows page 68

George Rogers Clark

Lt. Gov. Henry Hamilton

Father Pierre Gibault

Francis Vigo

"Pacane Miamis Chief"

"Wawiachton a Chief of Poutcowattamie"

"Old Baby Ouooquandarong"

"A Jibboway Indian"

"Indian of the Nation of the Kaskaskia"

"Indian of the Nation of the Shawanoes"

"The Allies—Par nobile Fratrum!"

"Shelb — ns sacrifice"

The Wabash River at Vincennes

Ezra Winter murals at the George Rogers Clark Memorial

George Rogers Clark Monument at the University of Virginia

George Rogers Clark Memorial

Introduction

In the nineteenth century, George Rogers Clark received the unfortunate appellation "Conqueror of the Northwest." For a century it stuck. In 1921, Edwin Alderman, president of the University of Virginia in Charlottesville, not far from Clark's birthplace in Albemarle County, accepted a statue of a mounted Clark dubbed "Conqueror of the Northwest." He called it an "epic in metal and stone, of conquest and empire."[1] Alderman was following decades of American historiography. In his three-volume history of the American movement westward, Theodore Roosevelt titled his chapter on Clark's Illinois campaign, "Clark's Conquest of the Illinois, 1778."[2] William English, then president of the Indiana Historical Society, followed Roosevelt and titled his two-volume history of Clark's role in the American Revolution *Conquest of the Country Northwest of the River Ohio, 1778–1783 and Life of Gen. George Rogers Clark*, when it was released in 1897.[3] As Alderman's interpretation of history and the statue went out of fashion, so too did George Rogers Clark. One professor called the "conqueror" moniker "absurd."[4] The University of Virginia eventually removed the statue after protests of its depiction of Native Americans—a depiction that reflected popular attitudes prevalent at the time of its dedication.[5]

Neither the triumphalist version of Clark or his twenty-first-century dismissal reflect the remarkable campaign he led in 1778–1779 to wrest political authority in the Illinois Country from the British and place it in the hands of the new United States, specifically, Virginia. Clark mostly succeeded in the former, but replacing British with American flags over Illinois Country forts ultimately did not achieve the ends Clark sought. The land north of the Ohio River was too vast, too sparsely populated, too weakly governed, and too contested for any power to consider it "conquered." To assess events by those standards, however, is to load too much of a burden onto the campaign or the shoulders of a twenty-six-year-old militia officer. When he set out for the Mississippi in 1778, George Rogers Clark's goal was to relieve the military pressure on Kentucky's nascent settlements from British-allied Native Americans by taking the war to them and creating a threat to the western focus of Britain's power in Detroit.

Tactically, Clark succeeded brilliantly. With just 150 volunteers, he paddled, rode, and walked from the Appalachian Mountains to the Mississippi through all kinds of weather to seize the largest white settlements in the *Pays des Illinois*, the Illinois Country. Combining speed and surprise with a mastery of psychological warfare, skill at maneuvering the political gaps among various groups, and a healthy dose of luck, the small force accomplished the unexpected. Then, when the British lieutenant governor for Quebec at Detroit, Henry Hamilton, put off his planned offensive against Kentucky and Pittsburgh to counter Clark, the American responded quickly and turned the tables, mobilizing local resources and instead defeating and capturing the lieutenant governor. In the process, Clark established for himself and his men a reputation for ferocity that amplified the impact of the tiny military forces available to the American cause in the Trans-Appalachian theater. The Illinois Country remained in American hands for the rest of the war.

Strategically, however, the Illinois campaign was more disappointing. Native Americans in the Illinois Country quickly made peace, but they had not been among the more aggressive Native American nations raiding Kentucky or along the Appalachian frontier. Britain's strongest Native American allies around the Upper Great Lakes, Upper Wabash, Maumee, and Scioto Rivers took notice of Clark's presence, which they had to factor into their own calculations, but did not noticeably reduce their raiding activities. They certainly did not consider themselves "conquered." Indeed, for some of them, Clark's presence in the Illinois Country was as much an opportunity to extract better terms of trade and support from the British as a threat. While humiliating to the British, Hamilton's capture did not significantly weaken Detroit or undermine Britain's ability to continue the war on the frontier.

In the end, the title "Conqueror of the Northwest" reflected the times and attitudes of those who bestowed it. While the title might have appealed to Clark's human vanity, it did him no favors by divorcing the Revolutionary War leader and the Illinois campaign from the complexities of their age. *Till the Extinction of This Rebellion* seeks to set aside nineteenth-century triumphalism and twenty-first-century dismissiveness to consider the campaign in the eighteenth-century context in which it took place. It is primarily a military history, so the "who, what, where and when" of history figure prominently in the narrative.

However, Clark owed much of his success to a perceptive reading of the complex social, political, and economic currents that dominated life in the Trans-Appalachian frontier of the American Revolution. George Rogers Clark had few peers when it came to navigating those currents, particularly as they shifted in reaction to events. Those skills enabled him to wage a kind of psychological war, which contributed far more to his military success than the paltry military means at his disposal. The title of this book, *Till the Extinction of This Rebellion*, is a phrase Clark's adversary, British lieutenant-governor Henry Hamilton, used in his proclamation urging settlers to remain loyal to the Crown and fight the rebels as long as it would take. What ensued was a struggle that Clark fully understood sat on the edge of a knife. Clark responded with a determination to act "as daring as possible," a phrase he coined in his memoirs, to offset Hamilton's numerical advantages when counting his indigenous allies. It does not refer to recklessness, but a posture Clark consciously adopted for maximum psychological effect. For those reasons, we cannot truly appreciate the Illinois campaign without also reviewing the context in which it took place. That is where we begin to understand the "why." Although he got many, many things wrong, particularly as they related to Native Americans, he understood the French and British well enough to succeed. The book does not seek to pass moral judgment on any party involved in the campaign or war on the frontier, but to understand them the way they understood themselves and one another.

Firsthand accounts of the Illinois campaign are limited, in part, because it involved so few people. Historians must make considerable use of a long letter Clark composed to one of his patrons, George Mason, in 1779 and a draft memoir he started in the form of a long letter to a potential editor and publisher in 1791. Several volumes of his papers have been published, but nothing rivals the Mason letter and memoir. That said, Clark's reliability as a source is suspect. Although his contemporaneous records are very matter-of-fact, the letter and memoir were meant to burnish his reputation and, in the latter case, help recoup his finances. Bluntly, he needed to write a bestseller. That led to some embellishments and portions must be taken with a grain of salt. Editors later cleaned up his draft and released it to some acclaim, but I have quoted verbatim from Clark's 1791 draft to better capture his voice. Fortunately, Captain Joseph Bowman, one of Clark's company commanders, also kept a daily diary and noted many of the same events and conditions, albeit without the drama.

On the British side, Lieutenant Governor Henry Hamilton's memoir is also vital. Hamilton, however, had a vested interest in dehumanizing Clark and the Americans while downplaying his own culpability for British defeat. He had failures to explain and a reputation to protect. Just as Clark had Bowman, Hamilton had Captain Normand MacLeod, who kept a very straightforward diary that helps detail the British experience during the campaign. Correspondence and reports from other individuals help flesh out the story. But it should be remembered that the two men—Clark and Hamilton—whose first-person accounts are the most thorough, are unreliable narrators. I have not corrected original grammar or spelling for the sake of accuracy or inundated the reader with "[*sic*]."

The perspectives and experiences of women, the enslaved, and Native American are lacking. To the degree they were recorded at all, it was usually second- or thirdhand, translated, and written down by white men. At each intermediate step, varying agendas, attitudes, and simple mistakes entered the picture. So, we must make do with the information available and remember its limitations. Fortunately, modern historians have authored several in-depth studies of French and Native American communities, nations, interests, social structures, and behavior in the Illinois Country in recent decades. Their work gives us greater insight into the region, particularly the Native American side of the campaign, and helps explain the context in which Clark's strategy could succeed.

Naming conventions have shifted over the centuries. There is no agreed upon term to refer to the indigenous peoples of North America, so I use Indian and Native American interchangeably with respect to the larger collective because they are more familiar to modern audiences. At the same time, it should be remembered that Native Americans did not act collectively. Nations and the individuals within them pursued their own perceptions of their own interests at any given moment. Thus, it was not uncommon to find individuals making conflicting promises to differing sides at the same time. While whites at the time often saw this as racial duplicity and treachery, diplomats would recognize the behavior as common among European states in the face of changing circumstances and interests.

Individual tribal names can also be perplexing. Native American nations were often culturally and religiously defined before they were geographically or politically defined. The latter two aspects of group cohesion were more readily subject to change as leaders gained or lost influence and tribes moved from place to place. Europeans and white Americans often struggled with these more fluid characteristics and sought to apply concepts with which they were more familiar to understand groups. It guaranteed a loss of nuance. Whites tended to reach for familiar words borrowed from elsewhere to describe individual tribes or clans. Thus, for many white Americans the Haudenosaunee of the eastern Great Lakes became the "Iroquois," a French name, or the Six Nations. The diverse Anishinaabeg of the western Great Lakes became the Ottawa/Odawa, Potawatomi, Chippewa/Ojibwe, Nipissing, Mississauga, or some variation thereof. The Indians who dominated the area of Clark's Illinois campaign are generally known as the Peoria, Illinois, or Illini, a confederation of the Peoria, Wea, and Kaskaskia Indians. The dividing lines were not quite so clear as any of those designations assume, and they evolved over time as historians applied new names and categorical descriptions. For continuity between the narrative and source material, I employ the more frequently used names as they were understood by whites at the time but strive to use a more appropriate Native American name, when possible, without introducing too much complexity. Inevitably, it means repeating some misperceptions made by whites living in the area because that is how they understood people and events, but I attempt to draw attention to those errors.

I refer to those rebelling against the British Crown as Americans and those remaining loyal to it as the British or English. As is the case with Native Americans, those broad categories are too confining. Many who fought for the British were born in the colonies and many who fought for the Americans were born overseas. The broad categories also leave out the French, who had moved into the area long before British victory in the French and Indian and War gave nominal authority of the region to the British, at least in European and American minds. For that matter, the French in the area had intermarried with Native American tribes for decades. The result was a hybrid of people and identities who were multiracial and comfortable across cultures, but generally understood at the time to be "French," which was often their first language. So, the designation is more cultural than national. Even then, many culturally French individuals fought on the British or American sides. To complicate matters still more, some French people in the Illinois Country lived on the Spanish side of the Mississippi and/or switched sides more than once. When I refer to the French, I generally mean culturally French communities in the Illinois Country. Readers will, I hope, be patient with syntactical imprecision when it comes to the melting pot of the eighteenth-century Illinois Country.

Ultimately, this book is about the military operations of George Rogers Clark and Henry Hamilton, so the reader will be best served by understanding people and events through their biased and limited perceptions, which I identify in the text or notes. Those very biases and limitations affected their decision making and the outcome of the campaign.

Prologue

Henry Hamilton, the lieutenant governor of Quebec at Detroit, eagerly opened his latest packet of correspondence, including from the provincial governor of Quebec, Major General Guy Carleton. Outside Fort Detroit's walls, representatives from dozens of Native American nations camped, cooked, talked, ate, drank, smoked, and considered events across the American frontier. Their varieties of body paint, decoration, jewelry, feathers, fabrics, and blankets were a riot of colors signifying different roles and tribes. They only compounded the cacophony of sounds, languages, dialects, garment styles, cultures, and races that characterized Detroit's polyglot population: French, British, American, frontiersmen, traders, merchants, farmers, sailors, slaves, and even an occasional Spaniard from across the Mississippi. Some of the Indians had been there for weeks after responding to Hamilton's call for a grand council. They were eager to go home, but Hamilton prolonged their stays, waiting for word from higher authority.

Hamilton and Carleton both had ample experience in the American colonies, but they did not get along. The two disagreed over policy and what to do with the Indians in the West. Simply, Hamilton wanted to employ them in "making a Diversion on the Frontiers of Virginia and Pennsylvania."[1] For his part, Carleton was more reluctant. Indian warfare was brutal, could discredit the British cause, and do more to alienate Americans from the Crown than it might achieve. So, the two men left the issue to London and the king.

Eventually, the king decided. Things had changed after two years of war and his government was more willing to use heretofore repugnant tools. To support General Burgoyne's 1777 offensive from Canada, Lord George Germain, secretary of state for the colonies, informed Carleton, "It is the King's Command that you should direct Lieut. Governor Hamilton to Assemble as many of the Indians of his District as he conveniently can, and . . . employ them in making a Diversion and exciting an alarm upon the frontiers of Virginia and Pennsylvania."[2] Carleton simply forwarded Germain's letter to Hamilton. It arrived in the lieutenant governor's hands on June 16, 1777. He was ready.

Less than twenty-four hours later, Hamilton held a council with leaders from many of the Indian nations already gathered in the area: Odawa/Ottawa, Ojibwe/Chippewa, Potawatomi, Huron, Wyandot, Miami, Shawnee, and Delaware.[3] He initially hid his reasons for calling the council, instead, methodically building up to his goal of getting the Indians to join the war. First, he reaffirmed their existing relationship and sounded out their attitudes and thoughts about the Americans. After a round of toasts to the king, he presented belts from the Iroquois Confederation, already engaged in military operations against the Americans. The belts ostensibly called on the western nations to support the king's government and honor past commitments to it. With the council well-lubricated, he boasted about British military success in the East. It was important to do. The western nations had just lost three wars to the British and their colonies, in part by choosing sides poorly: the French and Indian War, Pontiac's War, and Dunmore's War. It was critical they pick a winner this time. Fourth, he reminded them of perfidies committed by settlers and accused the Americans of having widespread ambitions to seize land occupied by the Indians. Afterward, he revisited the relationship between the western nations and the Iroquois, who claimed suzerainty over them and the sole power to make decisions about war and peace. Hamilton indicated that the Iroquois would permit the western tribes to go to war and had done so themselves. It was a touchy subject for the western tribes, who had been building their own group identity outside the control of the Iroquois for years and had indeed decided matters of war and peace on their own, usually without Iroquois approval. He concluded by telling the gathered leaders that he would inform them of his ultimate intent at a later date, after they met to consider his words.

It was a well-measured diplomatic performance. Hamilton's presentation did not order the Native Americans to go to war. Such was beyond his power, and he acknowledged it, although the government in London might not. Instead, he had given them reasons to join the war on the British side, which some of the more militant among them had already done. His intentions were obvious, but he did not try to stampede the Indian leaders into a rash decision. It was a de facto recognition of their authority and decision-making process that many Englishman—and more than a few Americans—did not understand.

Hamilton eventually confessed his intentions: to put the hatchet into the hands of the Indians while announcing his expectation that they would obey the orders of the king. Then, he recommended they go to war. Displaying a symbolic hatchet, he sang the war song, which his deputy and several gathered British officers joined. It was rumored among Americans that the lieutenant governor even donned native garb and painted himself for war, as the Indians did.[4] Eventually, the assembled tribal leaders joined the governor and his officers, agreeing to make war on the Americans. With that, Hamilton held a great feast for the Native Americans gathered around Detroit and invited leaders from each tribe to meet separately at his house, most likely to suggest frontier targets and ensure that British officers could coordinate tribal activities. Thus, he had unified them in the cause of war, but divided them to work out the details, making the best deal he could with each tribe. He also wanted to assign officers in British service to each tribe and raiding party as a way of trying to limit atrocities against women and children, which he reminded the Indians was important to the king. Working out the specifics took several days and required more feasting and, although he did not mention it in his report, alcohol. Hamilton took it upon the British government to make reparations for ill done by one tribe to another as a way of reducing friction among the various nations.[5] Although he was unpopular with the English and French residents of Detroit for his tactlessness, Hamilton clearly understood the importance of soothing ruffled feathers in coalition warfare.

By July, nearly three hundred warriors and thirty loyalist or British officers in fifteen parties had departed Detroit for the American frontier. In September, the lieutenant governor could report that some 1,050 Indian warriors were dispersed across the frontier, seven hundred of whom were equipped specifically by Hamilton.[6] During the multiday council, Hamilton crafted a proclamation:

Detroit, 24th June, 1777

By virtue of the power and authority to me given by his Excellency Sir Guy Carleton Knight of the Bath, Governor of the province of Quebec, General and Commandant in chief, &c. &c. &c.

I do assure all such as are inclined to withdraw themselves from the Tyranny and oppression of the rebel Committees, & take refuge in this Settlement, or any of the Posts commanded by his Majesty's Officers, shall be humanely treated, shall be lodged and victualled, and such as come off in arms & shall use them in defence of his Majesty against Rebels and Traytors, 'till the extinction of this rebellion, shall receive pay adequate to their former Stations in the rebel service, and all common men who shall serve during that period, shall receive his Majesty's bounty of two hundred acres of Land.

Given under my hand & Seal. God Save the King

Henry Hamilton

Lieutt. Govr: and Superintendent[7]

Hamilton had multiple copies printed to distribute across the frontier. On its face, the broadside seemed simple enough, but the most effective way of spreading the circular was via the raiding parties and British officers he was sending east and south.

Americans read the proclamation differently. Usually, they found it tacked to the frames of burned frontier homesteads or next to the mutilated bodies of victims from Indian raids. So, it was natural for frontier settlers and militia to view the proclamation as a declaration of all-out, merciless war.

CHAPTER ONE

Exciting an Alarm

George Rogers Clark was naturally charismatic. At six feet tall, he stood several inches above most of the men gathered for the June 6, 1776, meeting he had arranged. Broad-shouldered and moon-faced with auburn hair, Clark had a booming voice, a quick mind, and a restlessly entrepreneurial mindset that could be used for inspiration, persuasion, or intimidation depending on the circumstances. Born in 1752 in Virginia's Albemarle County, not far from Thomas Jefferson's birthplace, Clark's family moved with the tides of violence on the Virginia frontier. When he was five, the family relocated to Caroline County, farther from the assaults on Virginia's populated borders during the French and Indian War. He briefly attended school in the home of Donald Robertson, more famous, perhaps, for teaching James Madison at the same time. Clark's formal education did not last long, and he left at fourteen after just a year of instruction. Instead, Clark took up surveying, a frequent path to economic advancement pursued by those with little access to capital or formal education. Surveying took him west and gave him wide-ranging experience on Virginia's frontier. In 1774, he became a captain in the Virginia militia during Dunmore's War between the colony and the Shawnee opposing white settlement in Kentucky. After the war, he became a fixture on the Ohio River and in Kentucky. Most importantly, in his first twenty-four years, Clark acquired the toughness and skills for living on the frontier while developing latent talents for influencing and leading people. On that day in 1776, he intended to do both.[1]

For years, travelers, campsites, and isolated farms west of the Appalachians and along the Ohio River had experienced episodic attacks from Native Americans not reconciled to the Treaties of Fort Stanwix (1768), Camp Charlotte (1774), or Sycamore Shoals (1775), which ostensibly opened western Pennsylvania, Virginia, and Kentucky to white settlement.[2] Virginia's victory in Dunmore's War in 1774 had not stopped them. The American Revolution's outbreak only worsened the situation. Internal divisions, conflicting claims of authority, disputes over land ownership, and disagreements over loyalties hampered the ability of settlers in three tiny Kentucky towns—Harrodsburg/Harrodstown, Logan's Station/St. Asaph's, and Boonesborough—to establish a rational defense. One faction of settlers claimed allegiance to, and land rights from, Virginia. The other clung to suspect proprietary claims made by the Transylvania Company, a private venture led by a North Carolinian, Richard Henderson.

Clark, by then a major in the Virginia militia, wanted to organize a vote and petition the Virginia Assembly for military support, citizenship, and representation, but he could not admit it beforehand and left the purpose of the meeting vaguely defined until it occurred. He recalled, "the reason I had for not publishing what I wished to be done, before the day, was that the people should not get into parties on the subject; and, as everyone would wish to know what was to be done, there would be a more general meeting."[3] Clark's short admission tells us something about how he managed people: keep them in the dark about his intentions until he was prepared to rush to decision. In short, surprise was a political tool in Clark's hands. As a deputy surveyor of the Virginia-based Ohio Company, Clark also had a personal interest in the outcome.

Ironically, Clark was delayed and arrived too late to win his case. The divisions he feared reared their heads and the Kentucky meeting did not resolve the split between the Virginia and Transylvania factions, but attendees agreed to learn what Virginia might offer. In short, Clark's delay meant deferring a decision about allegiances, but a consensus on approaching Virginia first for support. It was a partial victory for the lanky Virginian. Clark and Captain John Gabriel Jones were elected as delegates to negotiate terms for bringing the Kentucky settlements into Virginia as a new county.[4] The petitions to the Virginia Assembly were as much sales pitches as they were pleas for assistance, but it was a start. Should Virginia assert its interests and sovereignty over the region, the Transylvania Company's claims would not stand. Simply, among whites a state's assertion of sovereignty trumped a private company's claims rooted in a questionable treaty with the Cherokee. Of course, should Virginia's terms prove unsatisfactory, Kentuckians might still opt to stick with Henderson's Transylvania Company and its evolving plans to establish a new colony. (Those plans could change as word of the Declaration of Independence and the war's progress reached the frontier.)

When he arrived in Williamsburg, Clark found an embryonic state government led by a three-man council and Governor Patrick Henry. Kentucky was not a high priority, although most of Virginia's political leaders believed their state's claims on the West took precedence.[5] The council simply agreed to provide Kentucky with five hundred pounds of gunpowder, which Clark could collect at Fort Pitt. Dissatisfied, he left, only to be called back and given another opportunity to make his argument. So, in October, Clark and Jones pitched bringing Kentucky formally under Virginia's jurisdiction, again selling Kentucky's value to Virginia as much as pleading their own needs.[6] The two also stepped into a roiling argument between Richard Henderson himself and Colonel Richard Campbell of Fincastle County, Virginia. The county's borders nominally extended to the Mississippi and encompassed the settled areas of Kentucky. Neither, of course, wanted to recognize the Kentucky settlements as the heart of a new Virginia county.

While the politicians and businessmen in Williamsburg argued, Kentucky's settlements remained vulnerable. With no immediate progress in sight, Clark set out for Fort Pitt to recover the promised gunpowder and deliver it to Harrodsburg, the largest town in Kentucky. He suspected some of the Native Americans at Fort Pitt of being spies aware of his purpose. Rather than waiting, he displayed a penchant for moving quickly before potential enemies could act against him. Clark and Jones gathered seven men—all they could find in a pinch—and set out in a small boat, paddling hard for the Kentucky River. Confirming that Indians were on the river behind them and believing they were in pursuit, Clark and his men went ashore and buried their supplies in several different locations at the mouth of Limestone Creek (today's Maysville, Kentucky), hoping to hide the caches.[7] Then, they paddled farther downriver, set their boat adrift, and headed overland to the Kentucky settlements to raise a force sufficient to collect the buried supplies.[8] After a few miles on the road to Harrodsburg, the group split up. Jones and four men remained behind. Shortly after Clark departed, a few local militia encountered Jones and his group. They set out to recover the supplies but were ambushed en route on December 25. Jones was killed while three others were killed or captured.[9] Nevertheless, a party from Harrodsburg successfully recovered Clark's supplies and returned them to the Kentucky settlements. His first exercise in community leadership was a success.

While Clark was lobbying Virginia authorities for support, British officials were debating the role they wanted Native Americans to play in the war. Lord Germain, the former Viscount Sackville, might inform Carleton it was the king's order to "make a diversion," but the order to Hamilton was made in the king's name on behalf of the British government. In the war's first years, both the British government and Continental Congress sought neutrality among those Native American nations they feared might join the other side and friendship from those nations that might become allies. An uneasy and imperfect peace resulted, while Native Americans debated their own reactions to the growing rebellion.[10]

Part of Britain's policy was forced on it. The initial American advance into Canada interrupted Britain's ability to provide Native Americans with the trade goods they wanted, most notably firearms, gunpowder, and ammunition. Britain's defeat of the American campaign in 1776 reopened those supply lines, giving frontier officials like Henry Hamilton more diplomatic tools. Thus, the opportunity to stimulate a general Indian war presented itself.

The reasons to do so came later. George Washington's year-end successes in 1776 in the Battles of Trenton and Princeton led to a general reappraisal of the strategic situation and the adoption of a new strategy for 1777. Dividing New England from the mid-Atlantic colonies by advancing through the Champlain and Hudson Valleys was always on the British menu of strategic options. In London that winter to attend to his affairs and consult with the government, General John Burgoyne developed a detailed campaign plan that included "a thousand or more savages" with the main army on the Hudson River and a diversionary campaign from Oswego to the Mohawk River. Of necessity, both had to contain sizeable Native American contingents from the Iroquois Confederacy and the Great Lakes farther west.[11] Lord Germain's letter to Carleton directing that Lieutenant Governor Hamilton employ Native Americans reflected the application of that change to the western theater.

The policy was controversial among Englishmen, both in the colonies and in Britain. During the Seven Years War, when the American colonies were part of the British Empire in relatively good standing, the French had supported Native Americans in open warfare against the British colonies. British citizens were well aware of the brutal nature of frontier warfare, which the government and press played up for propagandistic reasons. During the revolution, opponents of the North Ministry heaped opprobrium on the government for its change of course and mobilization of Indians to suppress the rebellion. Edmund Burke famously derided an address Burgoyne delivered to his Native American allies, satirizing it so effectively that Lord North himself reportedly broke down in laughter.[12] Even after Germain's letter arrived in Hamilton's hands, Captain Edward Abbott, a lieutenant governor of Quebec originally assigned to Vincennes on the Wabash River, deplored the practice of employing Indians in the war. Having departed his post for lack of gifts to use in discussions with the local tribes, Abbott wrote Carleton from Detroit and argued that Native American attacks would only force frontier settlers into the cause of rebellion. He wrote, "Your Excellency will plainly perceive the employing Indians on the Rebel frontiers has been of great hurt to the cause, for many hundreds would have put themselves under His Majesty's protection was there a possibility: that not being the case, these poor unhappy people are forced to take up arms against their Sovereign . . . it is not people in arms that Indians will ever daringly attack; but the poor inoffensive families who fly to the deserts to be out of trouble, and who are inhumanely butchered sparing neither women or children. . . . I will be bold to say, their keeping a neutrality, will be equally (if not more) serviceable to us, as their going to war."[13]

To modern ears, Abbott's protestations might sound terribly naïve, but throughout the war British officials continually overestimated loyalist support for their cause. Still, they were not chimerical on the frontier. Lord Dunmore's former agent in Pittsburgh had led a plot to mobilize western loyalists to the British cause at the war's beginning; several prominent frontier leaders defected to the British in 1778; and, as late as 1782 American officials at Pittsburgh continued to suspect various groups of locals of planning to go over to the British side. In short, Abbott's fears of a counterproductive policy were well within reason. Nevertheless, the die was cast in 1777 and events had taken on a life of their own. Although Britain's change in Indian policy was decided in London, Henry Hamilton became the focal point of American animosity on the Ohio frontier and Americans blamed the lieutenant governor for the war unfolding west of the Appalachians.

In truth, Native American raids west of the Appalachians began even before Hamilton received his instructions. By the spring of 1777, settlers along the Kentucky River were already in dire straits. In March, the Shawnee war captain Black Fish led a large party across the Ohio, frequently attacking Harrodsburg and Boonesborough.[14] Skirmishes were brief, but often bloody and occurred near the forts all summer. It was dangerous to venture beyond a town's walls.[15] Clark's diary that winter and spring is rife with entries detailing periodic attacks. Shortly after Jones and most of his men were killed attempting to retrieve Clark's gunpowder, an Indian raiding party attacked McClelland's Fort, wounding four men, two of whom later died. Inhabitants later abandoned the fort. On March 7, a body of Indians attempted to cut a few men off from Fort Harrodsburg. The Native Americans lost one man, whom the defenders scalped. For their part, the whites lost one man from his wounds, and a few cattle. But, so far from resupply in the East, a thin line divided full bellies from starvation. Lost cattle mattered. The same day, Indians killed one man and wounded another at Boonesborough. Eleven days later, a small party of Indian raiders killed another man within two miles of Harrodsburg. And, as March came to a close, a large Native American war party attacked "Stragglers" near Fort Harrodsburg, but outside its walls, killing and scalping at least one man and capturing another.

April started out relatively quietly but, on the twenty-fourth, a large war party attacked Boonesborough, killing one and wounding three inhabitants. Five days later, more Indians attacked the fort at Harrodsburg, killing one. They were back to shoot at the fort on May 6, but did no damage. A large party attacked Boonesborough again on May 23, bringing the fort under fire for a day and a half, attempting to start fires three times and wounding three men. On May 30, Indians attacked Logan's Fort, killing one man and wounding two more, at least one of whom died within a few days. In early June, several messengers failed to appear when expected, and Clark assumed they had been killed en route. On the twenty-second, Barney Stagner was famously killed and beheaded just a half mile from Fort Harrod's walls. The same day, someone took a few shots at Fort Boonesborough, but did not injure anyone.[16] The numbers might seem slight, but the American population in Kentucky in 1777 was fewer than five hundred people. Things only escalated after Hamilton started more actively supporting and coordinating raids.

The problem was straightforward for frontier communities. Kentucky's forts and the collection of houses inside their walls were not self-sustaining.

The farms, homesteads, and livestock upon which people relied for their survival, not to mention hunting opportunities and supply routes to the east, all lay well outside a fort's walls. Routine tasks required leaving the fort, where individuals were isolated and vulnerable to attack. Taking refuge inside the walls meant that farms went unworked and were vulnerable to devastation in a raid. Kentucky's inhabitants faced ruin at best, starvation at worst. Clark summed up the dilemma:

> [the attacks] ware continual and frequently sevear whin compared to our small forces the Forts ware often attacted (policy seem to have Required that the whole should be imbodied in one place but depending on Hunting for the greatest part of our provitions forbid it) no people could be in a more alarming situation detached at least two Hundred miles from the nearest settlement of the State surrounded by numerous Nations of Indians each one far superior in number to ourselves and under the Influance of the British government and pointedly directed to destroy us as appeared by many Instruments of writing left on the brest of people Kiled by them.[17]

The situation was bad enough that he feared some in Kentucky would seek British protection. Brigadier General Edward Hand, the new commander of the Western Department, shared the concern. He wrote the commander in chief, George Washington, in September, "Gouvernor Hamilton's Proclamation together with his Agents have gaind many of the Infatuated Inhabitants even of this remote Corner to the British Interest."[18]

Hand planned to conduct a raid on suspected British supplies at the Cuyahoga River to the north. He informed the settlements in Kentucky. At the end of the year, Colonel John Bowman, the senior Virginia militia officer in Kentucky, replied:

> [the] news gives great satisfaction to the poor Kentucky people, who have these twelve months past been confined to three forts, on which the Indians made several fruitless attempts. They have left us almost without horses sufficient to supply the stations, as we are obliged to get all our provisions out of the woods. Our corn the Indians have burned all they could find the past summer, as it was in cribs at different plantations some distance from the garrisons, & no horses to bring it in on. At this time we have not more than two months bread,—near 200 women & children; not able to send them to the inhabitants; many of those families are left desolate, widows with small children destitute of necessary clothing.[19]

In Detroit, Lieutenant Governor Hamilton agreed. Exchanging letters with a French correspondent, he wrote around the same time, "As for the news—the rebels have furnished more blood than one could believe existed in a body so recently formed. For neophytes, they show themselves to be excellent martyrs . . . the Indians have done their duty perfectly; I cannot praise them enough."[20] Kentucky and the Trans-Appalachian frontier were in dire straits.

Virginia's government was not indifferent to Kentucky's needs in 1777. It took several steps to improve its war footing in the West. It arbitrarily resolved the debate between Henderson's Transylvania Company and Fincastle County by dissolving the county. Three new ones replaced it: Montgomery, Washington, and Kentucky.[21] Although he didn't know it, Clark had achieved the goals he set for himself when he called that June 1776 meeting. Henderson contested it and it took years to sort out individual land claims, but Virginia's assertion of sovereignty over Kentucky left the Transylvania Company and its preferences high and dry.

Because Kentucky County's population was so small, reinforcement for the beleaguered settlements would have to come from elsewhere in Virginia. In March, the state council decided to permit up to one hundred men from Botetourt and Montgomery Counties to assist the settlements in Kentucky County. In June, John Todd, newly elected delegate from Kentucky County to the state legislature, arrived in Williamsburg and convinced it to authorize another 150 men.[22] (Todd was the future Mary Todd Lincoln's great-uncle, although he died long before she was born.)[23] While Todd pled his case to legislators, Colonel Bowman was already recruiting east of the Appalachians. He returned to Kentucky in August with one hundred men, whom he distributed among the three principal settlements: Harrodsburg, Boonesborough, and St. Asaph's/Logan's Fort.[24] It was a welcome addition. Kentucky's population was still small but growing with people eager to obtain their own land.[25]

In Detroit, Hamilton was just beginning his grand council with Native Americans, which would dramatically increase the threat to whites moving into the area. The modest steps Virginia and Kentucky County had taken would not be enough. George Rogers Clark knew it. He had a plan.

CHAPTER TWO

An Expedition of Great Consequence

Spring 1777 to Spring 1778

*I*n *1768, Britain's legendary superintendent* for Indian affairs, Sir William Johnson, and the Iroquois Confederation agreed to the Treaty of Fort Stanwix, in which the Iroquois ceded lands south of the Ohio River to the British. The Iroquois did not live there, but claimed suzerainty over the Shawnee who hunted the region. Naturally, the Shawnee resented the Iroquois for signing the treaty and the resulting white influx. That resentment led to cross-river raids and counter raids and growing tensions between the Shawnee and whites. They eventually broke into open warfare during Dunmore's War, in which Virginia's governor, John Murray, sought to enforce Virginia's claims south of the Ohio River under the Treaty of Fort Stanwix. British diplomacy largely isolated the Shawnee in that war, which meant it was a contest between the colony of Virginia and the Shawnee, which the Virginians nominally won. Black Fish was a Shawnee war chief, or captain, in that war. He remained unreconciled to the peace established at Camp Charlotte, in which the Shawnee technically accepted the influx of white settlers into Kentucky. For Black Fish, the turbulence of the American Revolution was an opportunity to renew the raids. Thus, he acted of his own accord in 1776 and early 1777.

Black Fish's position, however, was not universally shared among the Shawnee. Political authority was more fluid than whites understood. Designations like "chief" or "war captain" implied clear lines of authority and leadership that were simply lacking. Shawnee leaders achieved their positions of influence by building consensus and being recognized for the pursuit of an entire Indian nation's interest. Thus, leaders could not simply order a thing to be done or force compliance with decisions. One of the most successful Shawnee leaders was a man named Hokoleskwa, known as Cornstalk among whites. He was a member of the Mekoche division, which often took the lead in governance and civil affairs. Although he was a peacetime chief and opposed conflict in general, Hokoleskwa proved to be an excellent strategist and nearly defeated one of two columns of Virginians at the Battle of Point Pleasant during Dunmore's War.[1]

Having made peace at Camp Charlotte in 1774, Hokoleskwa spent 1775–1777 attempting to maintain Shawnee neutrality, but as events progressed, his influence waned. To complicate matters further, British officials encouraged the Shawnee to side with them in the growing conflict with their American colonists. It was an irony surely not lost on Hokoleskwa, who could rightly reply that he was working to maintain a peace that the British had forced upon the Shawnee after defeating them in Dunmore's War. With Hamilton's June 1777 proclamation, Hokoleskwa finally lost his leverage.[2] Before the end of the year, he would be dead. Virginia militiamen seized him outside Fort Randolph on the Point Pleasant battlefield when he approached the fort to inquire about relatives being held prisoner inside. Militia captain John Hall had assembled men at the fort to support Brigadier General Hand's aborted campaign against Detroit. While hunting outside the fort, one of his men was killed by a raiding party. Hall and his men stormed back into the fort and promptly executed the Indian prisoners, including Hokoleskwa. In a twist of fate and a reminder of the intimacy of frontier violence, Hall was related to the dead militiaman, whose last name was Gilmore. In 1759, Hokoleskwa had led a raiding party into Virginia's Augusta County and murdered several members of the Gilmore family living on Carr's Creek.[3] Despite its considerable size, the frontier could be a small world, indeed.

Exactly when Major Clark of the Virginia militia conceived of invading the Illinois Country is unknown. Kentuckians spent most of 1777 improving defenses, procuring provisions, ambushing Indian war parties, burying the dead, and attending to the wounded. But Clark began to think about the big picture in his spare moments: "the whole of my time when not thus Imployed in Reflecting on things in Genl particularly Kentucky how it accorded with the interest of the United States." With that, he decided to set aside self-interest and dedicate himself to the fate of the republic and pursue his idea of the national interest.[4] It was a notion that George Washington shared. Clark was evolving from a frontier fighter and scout into a strategist. Although he may have exaggerated his commitment to the national interest and downplayed his self-interest in his memoir, Clark still thought in terms bigger than Kentucky, which set him apart from many of his fellow frontiersmen.

As early as April 1777 when Black Fish's Shawnee were raiding Kentucky, Clark sent Benjamin Linn and Sam Moore into the Illinois Country as spies. Linn had years of experience on the frontier, particularly among the Shawnee, Miami, Delaware, and Kickapoo, and spoke their languages well enough. He and Moore carried pelts to convince the locals at Kaskaskia on the Mississippi River that they were hunters looking to trade. The two returned in June after confirming that British regulars had abandoned the town to defend Detroit, leaving Kaskaskia's defenses in the hands of the local militia. A well-stocked fort stood near the town but lacked a regular garrison. The residents were a mixed bunch of French and English families, who traded extensively with the Indians, the Spanish at New Orleans, and the British at Detroit. In Clark's view, those supply lines were important to maintaining Detroit as an important British post. Linn and Moore also reported that the residents were very hostile to the American cause due to British propaganda, but also lacked "apprehension of danger from the [Americans.]"[5] Clark concluded they could be surprised and swayed to the United States once directly acquainted with Americans.[6]

Clark also relied on a group of merchants scattered throughout the region for intelligence about developments there.[7] Englishmen living along the Mississippi had already supported early American efforts to secure supplies from the Spanish side of the river. Representatives of eastern merchant companies, they had sought to patent land before the revolution, which the British governor, Thomas Gage, voided. Naturally, they were not fond of British constraints on their futures and sympathized with the American rebellion. Some went so far as to assist William Linn, Benjamin's brother, in his 1776 efforts to obtain gunpowder and supplies from New Orleans on behalf of the Virginia Committee of Safety.[8] Providing intelligence during the Linn-Moore mission was consistent with their earlier behavior, but their interests no doubt shaded what they relayed.

When Colonel Bowman returned to Kentucky in August with his reinforcements and the promise of more to follow, it was an opportunity for Kentuckians to change their approach to the war. Clark's thoughts had congealed around a general strategy that he planned to present to the Virginia government in Williamsburg. The major believed that Kentucky stood as an impediment to Indian raids farther east. In the broadest terms, the settlements were situated between the Cherokee to the south and the western tribes north of the Ohio. In Clark's analysis, eliminating the Kentucky settlements would make it easier for the British to unite their Indian allies and raid the frontiers farther east, forcing coastal authorities to divert serious resources to frontier defense: exactly the goal the British government had in mind.[9] On the other hand, patriots in Kentucky sat near the heart of British power in the West and could easily march north or south, providing a similar threat to Britain's hold in the west. Therein lay Kentucky's value to the overall American war effort. It was a perceptive view of the war and in Clark's mind made Kentucky a vital linchpin in America's future. For Clark, striking at the largest towns in the Illinois Country, as the area between the Mississippi and Wabash Rivers was known, would undermine the British hold on the region and create exactly the kind of threat he envisioned. He could cut Detroit's supply lines from the west and deprive the British of their Indian allies in the Illinois Country. It would have the added benefits of opening the Mississippi to more reliable trade between the Americans and Spanish on the western bank.

Clark inflated Kentucky's importance in the war and his analysis was faulty. It was too weak early in the war to serve as a springboard against Detroit. Later in the war, even as Kentucky's population grew rapidly, it was never strong enough to prevent significant Native American raids across the Ohio River, whether to Kentucky, Virginia, or Pennsylvania. Nevertheless, his thinking highlights his growing strategic sophistication. Kentuckians could not defend themselves by indefinitely ceding the initiative to the British or their Native American allies. Characteristically, Clark sought to change the situation by taking the offensive.

That put the towns of Kaskaskia and Cahokia on the Mississippi and Vincennes on the Wabash squarely in Clark's sights. He claimed that was the reason for sending Linn and Moore on their spy mission, meaning he already had the idea of invading the Illinois Territory on his mind in the spring of 1777, when the Kentucky settlements were hanging on by their fingernails and before Hamilton issued his proclamation.[10] Of course, he did not share his thinking with Linn and Moore or, for that matter, many in Kentucky. He planned instead to make his first pitch to the government of Virginia.

That November, Clark returned to Williamsburg to settle militia accounts and present a plan to Governor Henry and the Executive Council for waging war in the West.[11] Although Clark had already demonstrated a penchant for seizing the initiative, in Williamsburg he acted indirectly, laying the groundwork for his proposal by discussing his ideas with the state's elite, but without formally proposing it or revealing any interest in leading it. Simply, he wanted to create a buzz and bring Virginia's governing classes around to his way of thinking without making any formal demands on them. It was a demonstration of the art of political persuasion, which he may have learned after obtaining gunpowder at the end of 1776. Governor Patrick Henry, Thomas Jefferson, George Mason, and George Wythe, who were already predisposed to assert Virginia's power in the West and establish better communications with the Spanish on the west bank of the Mississippi, also likely advised him on whom to approach and how.[12] They had their own interests in the West, both for the interests of Virginia and their own personal finances. Clark was presenting them with an opportunity to make their own cases in the coffeehouses of Williamsburg. Having planted the seeds, Clark left and traveled to his father's home in Caroline County.[13]

It was a short visit. He was back in Williamsburg by December 10 formally proposing the Illinois campaign to Governor Henry and the Executive Council.[14] Henry, of course, was game, but unsure whether he could dispatch Virginia forces to the frontier for an invasion of the Illinois Country without the consent of the council. It was forthcoming on January 2, 1778, when the council formally advised the governor "to set on foot the expedition against Kaskasky with as little delay & as much secrecy as possible," approving 1,200 pounds payable to Clark, whom it promoted to lieutenant colonel and placed in command.[15] It left additional specifics to Henry's discretion.

Publicly, Henry simply ordered Clark to enlist volunteers in seven companies of militia for service in Kentucky under his command for three months after their arrival in Kentucky County. In secret, Henry ordered Clark to attack the British post at Kaskaskia.[16] The secrecy was necessary to achieve surprise, but it also meant that troops enlisting for service in Kentucky were unaware they were bound for the Mississippi. In naming Kaskaskia as the target of Clark's force, Henry explained that the cannon and military stores reportedly there would be valuable to Virginia and then directed the newly promoted lieutenant colonel to establish a fortified post at the mouth of the Ohio River, indicating that the governor's main purpose was to secure lines of communication and supply with the Spanish, rather than undermining the British fort at Detroit. (A few weeks later, he also wrote the Spanish governor at New Orleans, Bernardo de Galvez, stressing Virginia's desire to open the Mississippi and Ohio to navigation between the Americans and Spanish Louisiana, secured by building a fort at the mouth of the Ohio.)[17] After that, Clark was free to proceed as he saw fit, striking British targets on the Mississippi and throughout the region, meaning the next two largest towns: Cahokia on the Mississippi and Vincennes on the Wabash.[18] Given the small numbers and short enlistment, the governor did not expect Clark to attack Detroit. Finally, Henry directed Clark to "show Humanity to such British Subjects and other persons as fall in your hands," and to treat white inhabitants who demonstrated allegiance to Virginia as fellow citizens. "But, if these people will not accede to these reasonable Demands, they must feel the miseries of War, under the direction of that Humanity that has hitherly distinguished Americans."[19] War in the West, already and always brutal, was meant to be merciless.

Henry wasted no time putting Clark's campaign into motion. The same day he addressed his orders to the newly minted lieutenant colonel, he wrote Brigadier General Edward Hand, the Continental Army commander at Fort Pitt: "I have to request that you will please furnish Major G.R. Clark with boats sufficient for conveying seven companys of militia on an expedition of great consequence." He was vague about the purposes, other than to tell Hand, "A good understanding with [New] Orleans is a desirable object." He left it to Clark to provide Hand with additional information and ended with an apology: "I should have consulted you on the expedition, but time would not permit."[20]

The governor was silent on the Native Americans living in the Illinois Country. Instead, Henry's political allies—Wythe, Mason, and Jefferson—addressed the relationship between the upcoming Illinois campaign and the region's Indians: revenge and land. Noting Indian attacks across the Virginia frontier, they wrote Clark on January 3, 1778: "it is intended to revenge the Injury & punish the Aggressors by carrying the War into their own Country." They went further and expressed their own thoughts that each soldier participating in the campaign should receive three hundred acres "conquered in the Country now in the possession of the said [hostile] Indians, so as not to interfere with the claims of any friendly Indians."[21]

Officers, of course, would receive larger grants, as was the custom. The three could not promise such a reward on behalf of the state, but their endorsement of it would go a long way toward establishing the claim. Virginia politicians were already debating how to utilize western lands to satisfy Virginia's war debts, compensate army volunteers, resolve conflicting claims, and open new opportunities for settlement. Mason even hoped to settle some of the prewar claims of the Ohio Company.[22] (At the end of the day, the assembly only granted two hundred acres for this initial enlistment; soldiers had to reenlist for the last one hundred acres.)[23]

Clark was charged with recruiting his own small army: 350 men. He dispatched five men throughout Virginia and the contested areas south of Pittsburgh.[24] William B. Smith had the greatest responsibility and was Clark's first commission as major on January 3. Clark had promised to recruit men from the frontier, so Smith traveled to the Holston region with 150 pounds and the responsibility of raising four full companies.[25] Clark had greater difficulty recruiting in the areas along the Ohio River south and west of Pittsburgh, which was already pressed by Indian raids. Moreover, Virginia's assertions of sovereignty conflicted with Pennsylvania's. So, he shifted his efforts eastward.

Governor Henry was unhappy with the breadth of Clark's activities. He expected the lieutenant colonel to recruit men from the western and frontier counties. Virginia had its own needs along the coast, defending its more established communities and claims along the Upper Ohio, providing men to the Continental Army, and keeping an eye on the enslaved populations throughout the state. An uprising was always high in the Virginia government's list of fears. An expedition to the Illinois towns along the Mississippi could prove exactly the diversion that the British sought. So, Henry chastised Clark before the month was out:

> I am under the necessity of expressing my Concern at your Conduct, well knowing that men inhabiting that part of the Country [Amelia County] are by no means proper to be employed in the Expedition which you are to direct; indeed you must certainly remember that you inform'd Me, that you expected to get Men enough to compleat the seven Companies partly in Kentuck & partly within the Carolina Line, and that if you shou'd fail in your Expectation, any Deficiency cou'd easily be made up in the frontier Counties in the neighborhood of Fort Pitt; the South Branch & the Frontier: I must therefore desire You to pursue your first Intentions, for by inlisting any men in the lower Counties, You will not only procure improper Persons, but you may also throw those

Counties into great Confusion respecting the Act of Assembly passed this Session for recruiting the Continental Army.[26]

To underscore the point, the governor informed Clark that men he enlisted in such a manner would not be exempt from the draft for the Continental Army. Meanwhile, on the Holston, Smith only succeeded in raising and outfitting one company of forty-four men by March, not the four companies Clark wanted, and was having trouble provisioning them. He had the sad duty to further inform Clark that back in Kentucky, Captain Daniel Boone and twenty-eight men were taken prisoner at the Salt Licks.[27]

Clark had hoped to begin his campaign quickly, but the difficulties in raising men forced him to wait. He had initially estimated his need at five hundred soldiers. Virginia had only authorized 350 and throughout the spring he had trouble meeting that number in Virginia proper. With the capture of Boone's party, he was unlikely to raise many more from Kentucky. Finally, in May 1778 he could wait no longer and set out from a rendezvous point on the Monongahela River for the Forks of the Ohio at Pittsburgh and then down the Ohio River, hoping to add to his force along the way before joining with some two hundred men he had planned to raise in the Holston area and Kentucky. He had all of 150 men with him and they still did not know they were ultimately bound for the Mississippi.[28]

CHAPTER THREE

Rebels on the Mississippi:
James Willing

George Rogers Clark was not the first American rebel to threaten Britain's hold on the Illinois Country or power on the Mississippi. Among Europeans, France had dominated the Mississippi for over half a century. As part of the 1763 Treaty of Paris ending the Seven Years' War, France transferred the area west of the Mississippi, including the critical port of New Orleans, to Spain. They became natural places for the Americans to look for the gunpowder, ammunition, and other war materiel that the Royal Navy and British diplomats were making difficult to obtain. (Native Americans, of course, actually dominated the region, but European monarchs and courts paid them little mind when drawing lines on a map.) In 1777, while Clark was eyeing the Illinois Country and the Mississippi, James Willing, who had gone west to make his own fortune, gave thought to the Lower Mississippi, particularly the town of Natchez on the east bank.

Willing was born in Philadelphia in 1751, the youngest son of Charles and Anne Willing. The family was prominent and well-off. Charles was a

London-born merchant who helped give Robert Morris his start in business, eventually naming him a partner. When Morris later became one of the revolution's chief financiers, James' oldest brother, Thomas, joined him raising funds by putting up his own private wealth against the public debt. He later went on to become president of the Bank of North America.[1]

James was the family's outlier. As the youngest, he had to make his own way and set out for Natchez in 1774. Within a few years, he had exhausted his resources with little to show for it and returned to Philadelphia in 1777. Likely exploiting his family connections, Willing arranged a naval captaincy from Congress, which authorized him to undertake an ill-defined mission on the Mississippi and return with supplies from New Orleans.[2] With little more than the commission in hand, he traveled to Pittsburgh, arriving on December 12 while Clark was in Williamsburg making his pitch to invade the Illinois Country. On the twenty-first, Willing promptly presented a list of his requirements to Brigadier General Hand, then commanding the post. It included one lieutenant or ensign, twenty-four regulars, a sergeant, a corporal, a ship's carpenter, ten additional volunteers, a boat with twelve or fourteen oars, forty stands of arms, 250 pounds of gunpowder with sufficient ammunition, one hundred pounds of iron, matches, paper, wadding, and sponges to support two swivel guns, and the range of additional equipment needed for men going to war. Hand, already besieged with the demands of supplying his own forces, must have groaned.

The congressional agent at Fort Pitt, George Morgan, could only support Willing's request. But, frustrated at the timing, he wrote Willing, "It is to be lamented that you had not been able to leave this 1st of October The Time I have so often pointed out to Individuals of Congress. You should now be about leaving Orleans to ascend the River & thereby secure your Passage & at one third the Expence of Provisions &c—I now dread the Issue."[3] Morgan, himself a merchant with extensive experience in the West, knew his subject. For his part, Willing also asked Hand to order sufficient supplies be delivered to Arkansas to support five boats with 100–125 men on the return trip.

With most of his men drawn from the 13th Virginia Regiment, Willing christened his large row bateau the *Rattletrap* and finally left Pittsburgh on January 10, 1778, just days after the Virginia Executive Council approved Clark's plan to invade the Illinois Country.[4] Ironically, the slapdash nature of Willing's mission began to trouble Congress in far-off Philadelphia when General Hand asked for guidance about fulfilling Willing's request for supplies on the return trip. Some suspected Robert Morris of arranging the whole thing without proper oversight and Hand's request for guidance was the first they heard of it.[5]

The *Rattletrap*'s passage down the Ohio did not go unnoticed by the British or their Native American allies. For that matter, one of Willing's first acts was to seize a large bateau from the Becquet brothers and relieve another trader, Mr. La Chance, of his cargo of brandy near the mouth of the Wabash River, not far from the British post at Vincennes. (The traders were Frenchmen who remained in Illinois after the French and Indian War transferred control to the British and were traveling on a British pass.) The Americans just missed capturing Philippe De Rocheblave, the senior British representative at Kaskaskia on the Mississippi, who was returning from a visit to Vincennes.[6] He informed the governor of Quebec, Major General Carleton:

> I learned upon my arrival at the beautiful [Ohio] River, the fifth of the present month, that two days ago a vessel had passed coming from Fort Pit, which had taken two brothers who under the passport of Mr. Abott [the British officer in charge of Vincennes] had gone to trade with the Indians. I learned the next day that they had also taken Mr. LeChance, officer of Militia at this place who left before me, going under my passport to journey to St. Vincennes. They took with the latter his childred, his effects and his negroes. They took likewise one of the two brothers of the first capture, with fifty packages of skins which they had, after making them understand that they should only put the blame on their passport and they wished to take Mr. Hamilton, Abbott, and myself. We discovered that, by their language, they were seeking to inspire a spirit of independence among the people. The ship is large, pointed and with quarter netting having, according to some of the energes, two cannon, and four, according to others, who say that two are masked, and forty soldiers, commanded by an officer from Philadelphia named Willing, who has three others under his orders. It is loaded with provisions.[7]

Along the way, Willing's force continued to grow. He was joined by two canoes and ten more men just before reaching the Mississippi.[8]

On February 19, Willing and the *Rattletrap* arrived off the plantation of Anthony Hutchins, a loyalist, just north of Natchez. Willing was almost home. He seized Hutchins and his moveable valuables. John Watkins told the story, testifying before a council formed by the governor of West Florida to consider the threat:

[A]t night Two Small Barges came to the landing place belonging to His Plantation . . . and landed a party consisting of about Forty Men Commanded by one Strodder Supposed to be a Lieutenant and one McIntyre said to be an Ensign in the Rebel Service. That these men came directly to his House and Seized four Persons named Robert Welsh, John Richmond Marshall Henry Earnest and John Earnest who were all in the employ of Colonel Stuart the Superintendent That the Rebels bound these people with Cords and repeatedly Swore that they would put them all to Death.[9]

After extensively interrogating and forcing Welsh to swear an oath of neutrality, the Americans took a rifle, two smoothbored fusils, and a pistol from him, allowed him his freedom, and removed the others to their boats. Watkins appears not to have been home during this episode, but the next day, Willing arrived in his bateau, accompanied by four canoes. He sent five men ashore, who made more threats and announced they were the advance party of a second force of two thousand men that would arrive in May.[10] (At this time, George Rogers Clark was recruiting up and down the Virginia frontier for an invasion of the Illinois Country in what was still supposed to be a secret mission.)

Then, Willing divided his men, dispatching the faster canoes under the command of Robert George and Thomas McIntyre to scout ahead. They arrived at Natchez late that day and immediately announced to the town's citizens that it was now under military occupation. Natchez was a multinational town of American, English, and French settlers who offered no resistance. The morning of the twentieth, Willing and the rest of his men arrived. He convened the town's population and announced the occupants were now prisoners of war and that he was contemplating seizing the town in the name of the United States. In truth, he had already done that, but Willing's mission required him to depart for New Orleans and he lacked sufficient forces to permanently occupy Natchez. The locals did not know that, so they worked out terms of surrender. One local wrote:

Our settlers were, with very rare exceptions, well disposed to the American cause. Willing was a good speaker, and he represented the case for the colonies, and the certainty of their ultimate success, in very persuasive terms. He assured us that five thousand American troops, under Gen. Clarke, were on their way to this quarter, to take possession and bring us under their jurisdiction, and all that Congress and he, their agent, required of us, was the oath of neutrality; which oath, when he concluded his address, was duly administered and freely taken; our people not being disposed to compromise themselves at that period of uncertainty and transition, by any overt act, on one side or the other, which might, in certain contingencies, be construed to their disadvantage.[11]

Essentially, they agreed to observe strict neutrality in the war provided their "persons, slaves, and other property of whatever description shall be left secure, and without the least molestation during our neutrality." Willing agreed, excepting the property of British officials, and limited protection to those who signed a pledge of neutrality. Still, he demanded provisions for his men, ordered all single men to join him—some did—and directed those who supported him to move to the Spanish side of the river.[12] For all intents and purposes, he was destroying the integrity of the community in which he had commercially failed and departed roughly a year before. Whether it was a demonstration of military success, an act of petty revenge, personal bullying, river piracy, or bravado is open to debate. But, the diversion, which lasted days, was not entirely in keeping with his mission of obtaining supplies from New Orleans.

Departing Natchez, Willing and his hodgepodge raiders proceeded to raid the plantations on the Mississippi below Natchez. He had acquired a second bateaux and still more men. His crews destroyed crops, killed cattle, burned houses, seized enslaved people, took hostages, and threatened worse to come. The plundered locals, who knew Willing, could only resent him. One such, William Dunbar, described the experience:

> About sun sett the Genl. Himself dropt down & put ashore at Walker's, where the scene that followed markes the nature of the man,/I had almost said Brute/The Houses were immediately rumaged & every thing of any value secured for the Commodore's use, after which the Heroick Captain ordered his people to set fire to all the houses & indigo works, which was accordingly done & they were quickly consumed to ashes—Twas not enough to pillage & plunder the man at whose house he had been often most hospitably entertained, his ruin must be compleated by a piece of wanton cruelty, from which the monster cou'd derive to himself no advantage ... the Houses of the English Gentlemen on the British side were plundered & among the rest mine was robbed of every thing that cou'd be carried away—all my wearing apparell, bed & table linen; not a shirt was left in the house—blankets, pieces of Cloth, sugar, silver ware, In short all was fish that came in their net, they destroyed a considerable quantity of bottled wine, tho' they carried away no liquor; ...

the orders given by their head were to drive down my negroes & if opposed by any one to shoot 'em down. . . .

Cap. Willing conceived the design of making his fortune at one Coup upon the ruin & destruction of his Old Friends & Intimates—His chief reason was that he had by his folly squandered a fortune upon the river & twas there he ought to repair it. In order to effect this, his hellish purpose, he recruited & collected together on his way down, all the vagabonds & rascalls he met with, of which kind the river is always full.[13]

Dunbar believed that Willing's force had reached two hundred men by the time he reached the Lower Mississippi. Ironically, Willing eventually provided Dunbar a pass to exempt him and his property from further seizures, "he being a frd to America." In all likelihood, Dunbar had also thrown in the towel and sworn the neutrality oath.[14]

Willing's next target was the town of Manchack upon which he descended "so rapidly that they reached the Settlements without being discovered."[15] On the twenty-third, Willing's advance parties captured the 250-ton British sloop *Rebecca*, with sixteen 4-pounders and six swivels.[16] It was a major coup. *Rebecca* was normally a merchant vessel but had been armed and sent upriver to contest the *Rattletrap*'s advance by protecting Manchack. Instead, her presence had strengthened Willing's force. Captured while lying against the levy opposite the town, she only had fifteen men aboard when an equal or superior force of Americans struck about 7:00 a.m.[17] With Manchack captured and the *Rebecca* renamed the *Morris*, Willing turned his attention to the end game at New Orleans, where he hoped to dispose of his booty and obtain supplies useful for the American war effort.

At New Orleans, the congressional agent, Oliver Pollock, was aware of *Rattletrap*'s advance and began preparing to dispose of the property Willing and his raiders had taken, a growing portion of which constituted enslaved people. He organized a small force under his nephew, Thomas Pollock, to go upriver and help Willing bring his vessels and cargo into port. Instead, Pollock and his men proceeded downriver, where they captured an English brig, the *Neptune*, eventually bringing her into New Orleans as a prize.[18] (The British would argue strenuously that *Neptune* and a private boat were not in fact legal prizes.)

Willing's eventual arrival in New Orleans created potential problems for the Spanish government and the local governor, Bernardo de Galvez. Spain was still a neutral party in the war. It conducted an extensive commerce across the river, with loyalists and rebels alike, and constantly had to contend with the British forces ensconced in the colonies of East and West Florida. Many of the loyalists had fled to the Mississippi's west bank seeking protection from Willing's flotilla. At the same time, an opportunity to weaken Britain in the Gulf of Mexico and enrich Spain presented opportunities. Galvez sensed them both. He had to thread the needle of pursuing Spain's interests at Britain's expense without causing a formal breach. His solution was to provide protection to the loyalists and disallow high-profile transactions with Willing. Instead, he would permit deniable commercial interactions with the Americans "which must take place quietly so that it cannot be proven that I know of this business, so as to avoid any quarrels or complaints by the Court of London on this matter."[19] Moreover, he assumed that British subjects under Spanish protection would liquidate their assets, particularly their enslaved workforce, at fire sale prices in order to return to Europe. This made human property a particularly lucrative target for Willing to seize, since that increased the likelihood that loyalists would sell them rather than lose them and the Spanish were always willing to purchase them. The result was to transform the last portion of Willing's original mission—obtaining supplies for the American war effort—into a campaign of slave trading.

Politically, protecting loyalists and permitting the Americans to profit while maintaining deniability of Spain's own role was a reasonable approach until the British sloop *Sylph*, commanded by John Fergusson, arrived on March 14. Fergusson was eager to press the British case against Willing and demand the return of captured property. Until that point, Galvez had been able to put off private petitions for relief. Fergusson's presence and communications were official matters that could not be so easily avoided. He eventually split the difference, requiring the return of some property, but quietly allowing the Americans to dispose of portions for cash.[20] Galvez had fewer qualms about permitting Willing to obtain the supplies he had originally been sent to purchase, yet also wanted that kept secret.

The British were not content to cede Willing's control of Natchez or Manchack. In addition to sending the *Sylph* to the Mississippi, they sent fifty men toward the latter town and successfully recaptured it from a tiny American garrison on March 19, killing two men and one woman, wounding eight or ten more people, and capturing another fourteen. Willing could not allow that to stand and sent his own detachment north to successfully retake the town. But, rather than garrison it, the Americans moved upstream, continuing to plunder English plantations and capture slaves.[21] The forces at his disposal continued to grow as locals joined him, perhaps more motivated by his riverine raids than any real identification with the American cause. Opportunists are often happy to join "armies" when the prospect of booty is high, and the risks low. The change indicates that Willing's mission had grown well beyond its original intent of securing supplies. Indeed, the congressional agent at Pittsburgh, George Morgan, had anticipated a rapid descent to New Orleans and a quick return when helping outfit the mission. But Willing's plundering successes had taken on a life of their own as more men flocked to his banner and he tarried in New Orleans.

Events at Manchack may have prompted Willing to fear for Natchez as well. Indeed, despite swearing an oath of neutrality, residents had sought assistance and a garrison from the British.[22] So, in April, Willing sent another detachment in that direction determined to ensure that the oath of neutrality was observed. Word spread among the residents that this latest American foray really intended to loot the town, entirely credible given their activities south of Natchez in February. So, they armed themselves and prepared to ambush the Americans at White Cliffs, below Natchez on the Mississippi. An attempt at a parlay failed, gunfire was exchanged, and the Americans withdrew and returned to New Orleans, with five men killed and several more captured.[23]

Willing was becoming an increasing pest for Galvez. He could not maintain any deniability about Spain's role in providing a de facto base of operations for Willing so long as Willing continued to raid the countryside. British merchants began demanding that Willing and Pollock be arrested and surrendered to the British.[24] It was one thing to quietly dispose of booty and enslaved people while Willing purchased goods locally for dispatch back up the Mississippi: a short-term affair that could be waved away with time. It was another to be dragged into an escalating conflict between the Americans and the British on the Lower Mississippi. Willing, however, remained, planning ever more operations in the region while continuing to dispute the matter of property he had seized, particularly the *Neptune* and a private boat taken on the Mississippi. In April, the British sloop *Hound* arrived to press the British case and the *Sylph* moved farther upstream. Rather than quietly disposing of Willing's seized property to the benefit of Spain, Galvez had to begin preparing New Orleans against a possible attack.[25] Hoping to reduce tensions, he required the British citizens who had sought and received his protection, and, more importantly, the Americans in town, to take an oath of neutrality. Most of the Americans did, but it was not enough.[26]

By May, while Clark was preparing to descend the Ohio River from Pittsburgh, the British had sufficiently mobilized their forces to establish a garrison of some two hundred men at Natchez and one hundred at Manchack, while the *Sylph*'s presence upriver controlled the Lower Mississippi. Willing had been effectively cut off from Pittsburgh. Galvez was hardpressed to defend his own town, key to Spanish Louisiana. He let American authorities know of his predicament:

> My Dear Sirs:
> The bearer of this letter will inform You of the Critical Situation in which I find myself with my neighbors, blocked from every side, and threatened with an attack if I do not turn over the prizes taken by Captain Willing, his person, Mr. Oliver Pollock, and several officers from his party considering the protection, asylum, and support I have given them a declaration of War. To force me to yield to their demands, they have placed two English frigates in front of the city, two corsairs at its back along Lake Pontchartrain, eight hundred English Royalists and Savages above the river in Natchez, another two frigates expected from Jamaica, and two companies of grenadiers arriving from Pensacola to Manchac. I find myself with only two hundred men for defense and so I do now know what will happen or what the results will be. Nevertheless, I have resolved to sacrifice everything before giving in to their demands and am not the least bit regretful that the occasion has arisen to prove my affection for You and my desire to serve you no matter the cost. May God protect [&c.]
> Berndo de Galvez[27]

Galvez's note can be read several ways. Literally, it was a pledge to the American cause, which exceeded his authority. No doubt, he and the letter's intended recipients knew this full well. The subtext, however, can also be read as a plea to the Americans to solve the problem of Willing for the Spanish. Bluntly, New Orleans was more useful to the Americans as a port in the hands of the Spanish than as a port seized by the British. Galvez, Smith, and Morris knew this as well. While war between Spain and Britain would serve American interests, Galvez's admission of weakness meant he had little to offer in the way of assistance. Pollock indirectly reinforced the message, confirming the Spanish weakness and proposing an American invasion at a time when the Americans themselves had little more to offer![28]

Oliver Pollock was having his own difficulties with the captain. Part of his duty was helping settle accounts for Willing and his men from the proceeds of sales from their seized property. Officers and sailors always over-estimated the value of the "prizes" they took while raiding. But, as Galvez had so astutely predicted, enslaved people made up a significant portion of the wealth that Willing and his men seized, depressing the market and enabling the Spanish to purchase them at a reduced price. As agent, Pollock was entitled to a cut of the proceeds. Worse from Willing's perspective, Congress claimed a portion. Thus, the American slave raids enriched Willing's crews less than they expected. Meanwhile, Galvez was reluctant to let Pollock dispose of high-profile property that promised to fetch a high price, such as the *Neptune*. Desertions were the result. Willing's forces began to shrink.[29] The captain exploded, writing the American agent: "My Men and Officers are discontented, myself displeased and the Governor himself highly dissatisfied with Your Conduct and what is of the most serious consequence My Men are deserting and the American Bank as it is termed is becoming Proverbially Ridiculous."[30] In the meantime, Pollock did his best to purchase and ship supplies to the Americans up the Mississippi aboard Spanish vessels, still taking advantage of Spain's technical neutrality and marginal control of the river's western shore. Pollock responded politely, but firmly, refuting Willing's accusations, but he was clearly ready to be rid of the captain, whose value to the American cause was rapidly declining.[31] He began looking for ways to get Willing and his men out of town.[32]

The Willing raid would affect Clark's mission in several ways. First, Willing's boasts that George Rogers Clark was following in his wake with five thousand men destroyed any secrecy that the lieutenant colonel and Virginia government hoped to attach to Clark's Illinois campaign, at least among British authorities along the Mississippi. Curiously, word of Willing's boasts seems not to have reached the Virginia government or George Rogers Clark—at least no one made the connection. At the same time, Willing's extended presence on the Lower Mississippi diverted British resources and attention to protecting settlements there. Fortunately for Clark, the primary attention came from British officials in the Floridas, not from Quebec or Lieutenant Governor Hamilton, who was comfortable dismissing the episode.

Third, it more deeply involved Spain and Governor Galvez in the American cause and created an opportunity for the Spanish governor to work more closely with the American agent in town, Oliver Pollock. The Spanish had supported initial efforts to obtain supplies from New Orleans in 1777 and 1778, but Willing's mission forced Galvez and Pollock to deepen their relationship, reducing the transaction costs of cooperation to support future American operations on the Mississippi. Thus, as Clark's campaign unfolded later in the year, Galvez and Pollock did not have to build a supporting logistical infrastructure from scratch. (Indeed, some supplies originally procured before Clark's mission began in earnest eventually made their way into the lieutenant colonel's hands, a welcome surprise.)[33]

Finally, Willing's success may have exacerbated local fears of Americans along the Mississippi. His actions had thoroughly ruined several British plantation owners by seizing goods, enslaved persons, and the plantation owners themselves. As Clark explained later, his small numbers would force him to rely on fear to dominate the psychological battlefield. Inadvertently, Willing had set the psychological stage for the drama about to unfold in the Illinois Country.

CHAPTER FOUR

No Part of the Globe: The Illinois Country

George Rogers Clark's battlefield was vast, stretching from Pittsburgh in the east to the Mississippi towns in the West, from the Kentucky settlements in the south to Detroit in the north. Of necessity, Clark narrowed his focus, but the wider campaign area still constituted over 180,000 square miles.[1] Clark set out from the Monongahela with roughly 150 men to seize it from the British.

Rivers and water routes dominated the region geographically, culturally, socially, and economically. They were the railroads and superhighways of the eighteenth century, making it possible to move relatively large bodies of men and supplies across vast distances. Although rivers, creeks, and portages were everywhere, several key waterways dominated the theater. In the north, the Great Lakes provided a reliable east-west water route connecting the Atlantic to the Upper Great Lakes. This made Detroit central in British strategy and the focus of American enmity toward the British. The north-south flowing Mississippi defined the western boundary. It was a critical means of communicating with the Spanish, who claimed the western shore, and provided access to the ocean through New Orleans. The Ohio ran east-west from Pittsburgh to its mouth on the Mississippi, dividing the battlespace between America's Kentucky settlements to the south and British/Indian territory to the north. Other key river routes flowed north-south into the Ohio all along its length. In the west, a series of rivers and portages dominated by the Illinois River connected Lake Michigan with the Mississippi. Ironically, the river and Native American nations that gave the region its name played only a modest role in the upcoming campaign. Instead, the Wabash River, which runs through Indiana and defines its southwestern border, became the third most important waterway in Clark's campaign, after the Mississippi and Ohio.

An English explorer, Thomas Hutchins, described the Ohio River Valley in fawning terms: "The country on both sides of the Ohio, extending South-easterly, and South-westerly from Fort Pitt to the Mississippi, and watered by the Ohio River, and its branches, contains at least a million of square miles, and it may, with truth, be affirmed, that no part of the globe is blessed with a more healthful air, or climate—watered with more navigable rivers and branches communicating with the Atlantick Ocean . . . or capable of producing with less labour and expence, Wheat, Indian Corn, Buck-wheat, Rye, Oats, barley, Flax, Hemp Tobacco, Rice, Silk, Pot-ash, &c. than the country under consideration."[2] Nicholas Cresswell, an English adventurer and would-be land speculator, traveled the river in 1775, a good portion of the way with Clark, whom he described as "an intelligent man." The river was populated with islands, often boasting hills on one bank and rich bottomland on the other, "wild yet truly beautiful" in his words.[3] On the way to Kentucky, where Cresswell hoped to acquire land, the party hunted bison, elk, and bear while feasting on catfish and turtle eggs. In other words, it was land worth fighting for, whether Frenchman, Englishman, American, or Indian.

The terrain lacks the kind of mountain chains that dominated the "back country" of the Appalachians. Instead, the Illinois Country between the Mississippi and Wabash was broken up by forests, rolling hills, ridges, low-lying bogs, ponds, gulches, creeks, gulleys, and rivers that regularly changed course and overflowed their banks. Consequently, water drained slowly and standing water could stretch for miles. Before European agriculture and the U.S. Army Corps of Engineers changed the region's geography, ecology, and hydrology, reducing the incidence of flooding, one could sometimes see the region as one vast "shimmering" plain of water populated by marsh birds, beaver, and fish broken up by hills and woodlots.[4] This too would dramatically affect the Illinois campaign when Clark and his little army needed to create surprise by marching away from the heavily monitored river channels. European-trained officers, even American officers accustomed to fighting along the Atlantic seaboard, might conclude that the terrain precluded military maneuvers; Clark had other ideas.

The key to the region was a crescent-shaped sliver of land along the Mississippi's east bank known as the American Bottom. It stretched from the mouth of the Illinois River in the north to the confluence of the Kaskaskia River in the south, bound on the west by the Mississippi and on the east by a series of bluffs, hills, cliffs, and ridges, generally several miles away from the river's edge.[5] Centuries of flooding had deposited rich soil throughout that crescent, which made it excellent for farming while the Mississippi readily connected it to Indian territories in the north and the Gulf of Mexico. Attracted by the land's bounty, Native Americans had lived in the region for centuries, including a cluster of nations collectively known as the Illinois. As Europeans explored the continent, French Jesuit missionaries predictably made their way to the American Bottom. Traders, merchants, farmers, and government officials soon followed, establishing towns all along the river and its tributaries. By the early eighteenth century, Cahokia, St. Philippe, Chartres, Prairie du Rocher, and Kaskaskia had grown up organically and haphazardly with French and Indians marrying and mingling for generations. Outlying settlements, notably St. Genevieve on the west side of the Mississippi, Peoria on the Illinois River to the north, and Vincennes on the Wabash River to the east defined an area known as *le pays des Illinois*, the Illinois Country. As elsewhere in the Western Hemisphere, local communities enslaved others. Thus, Clark's theater might be vast, but he believed it could be dominated by controlling the smaller area defined by the Illinois Country.

In 1751, a new French governor conducted a census and found that 350 French, 264 enslaved Black people, and 75 enslaved Native Americans resided in Kaskaskia. Another two hundred or so, including a small garrison and transients, were likely in town at any given time. The Kaskaskia Indian nation had established a separate town up the Kaskaskia River and was already in decline, partly due to constant warfare between the Illinois Nations and neighboring tribes.[6] (For comparison, Williamsburg, the capital of colonial Virginia, had an estimated 885 free and enslaved residents in the winter of 1747/1748, although Williamsburg's population would surge and decline with legislative sessions. Philadelphia, the largest town in the colonies, had a population of about fifteen thousand in 1750.)[7] The French

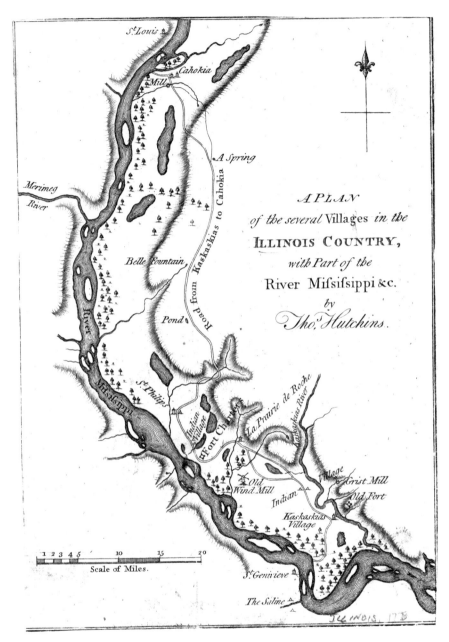

"A Plan of several Villages in the Illinois Country," by Thomas Hutchins, London, 1778. This contemporary map shows Cahokia at the top, followed down river by St. Philips [St. Philippe], Fort Charter [Chartres], Prairie de Roche [du Rocher], and Kaskaskia. (*Library of Congress*)

and Indian War largely passed *le pays des Illinois* by, but the towns there provided grain to French garrisons on the frontier and served as a reliable source of manpower to conduct raids against British settlements in the Appalachians.[8] France ceded the area to the British in the Treaty of Paris concluding the war and then Britain defeated most Indian resistance to its control in Pontiac's War.

The first British soldiers arrived in 1765, taking up position in an old French fort at Chartres. At best, British governance of the Illinois Country was indifferent. Seven different British officers served as commandant between 1765 and 1776 and continued conflict among Native American nations undermined the region's economic potential.[9] Some Frenchmen began moving across the Mississippi to territory ceded to the Spanish, where their lives continued virtually uninterrupted. Spaniards held the top posts, but the local power structure generally remained in the hands of local Frenchmen, who also provided the bulk of a rarely exercised militia.

In 1765, Captain Philip Pittman mapped the Mississippi, publishing his account and description of the region in 1770. He described a wealthy land along the American Bottom, paying particular attention to Kaskaskia:

> The village of Notre Dame de Cascasquias is by far the most considerable settlement in the country of the Illinois, as well as from its number of inhabitants, as from its advantageous situation; it stands on the side of a small river, which is about eighty yards across; its source lies northeast of the remarkable rock of Peorya, and it empties itself with a gentle current into the Mississippi, nearly two leagues below the village. This river is a secure port for large batteaux, which can lie close to its bank as to load and unload without the least trouble; and at all seasons of the year there is water enough for them to come up. . . . Another great advantage that Cascasquias receives from its river is the facility with which mills for corn and planks may be erected on it. . . . The principal buildings are, the church and jesuits house, which has a small chapel adjoining to it; these, as well as some other houses in the village, are built of stone, and, considering this part of the world, make a very good appearance.[10]

Besides noting its economic success, Pitman counted sixty-five families, plus merchants, other "casual" people, and enslaved people in town.

While Fort Chartres was well-located in the region, it was not well-located relative to the Mississippi's ever-shifting riverbank. Erosion forced the British to move to the abandoned stone Jesuit mission house in Kaskaskia, which they surrounded with a picket fence and dubbed Fort

Gage. A year later, in 1772, they largely abandoned that as well, pulling most troops back from the frontier to Detroit.[11] As the American Revolution consumed resources in the East, the last British official in Illinois, Captain Hugh Lord, departed in 1776, leaving behind Philippe-Francois de Rastel de Rocheblave, a local, as the default British authority in the region.[12] Rocheblave had no British troops, but only the indifferent local militia made up largely of Frenchmen, who had no love for the British or their new governor. (Captain Edward Abbott of the Royal Artillery arrived at Vincennes on the Wabash in 1777 as an Indian agent for the Ohio River but was recalled in 1778. Like Governor Carleton, he opposed a general Indian war.)[13]

Rocheblave was awkward in his new role. Born in France, he fought in the French and Indian War under Charles de Langlade, taking part in the French and Indian victory at the Battle of the Monongahela in 1755. He regularly led Indian raiding parties against English settlements throughout the war, apparently from Fort Duquesne. He escaped capture when the British subdued Fort Niagara and then largely faded away, making an occasional appearance along the Mississippi until he married at Kaskaskia in 1763.[14] When the British moved in, Rocheblave and his new wife decamped to the Spanish side of the Mississippi. He served his new masters as commandant at St. Genevieve. While there, he and his British counterpart engaged in a kerfuffle that escalated to their respective governors, General Thomas Gage in New York and Don Alexandro O'Reilly in New Orleans. The governors quashed the argument and that was the end of it. But, sometime between 1770 and 1776, Rocheblave returned to Kaskaskia as a British subject. Despite Rocheblave's dustup with his predecessor, Captain Lord not only made the decision to leave the Frenchman in charge as Britain's representative in town, but also entrusted him and Madame Rocheblave with the care of his English family.[15]

Despite, or perhaps due to, his sudden conversion, Rocheblave was a haughty official, treating the Frenchmen who had remained in Kaskaskia and the English merchants there as his inferiors. His behavior eventually provoked a reaction and the English locals petitioned Governor Carleton

Overleaf: "A new map of the western parts of Virginia, Pennsylvania, Maryland, and North Carolina," by Thomas Hutchins, London, 1778. The crescent-shaped American Bottom is at left along the Mississippi River in Illinois Country. The Wabash River converges with the Mississippi at the southern end of the Bottom. Fort Detroit is just south of Lake St. Clair above Lake Erie, top right. (*Library of Congress*)

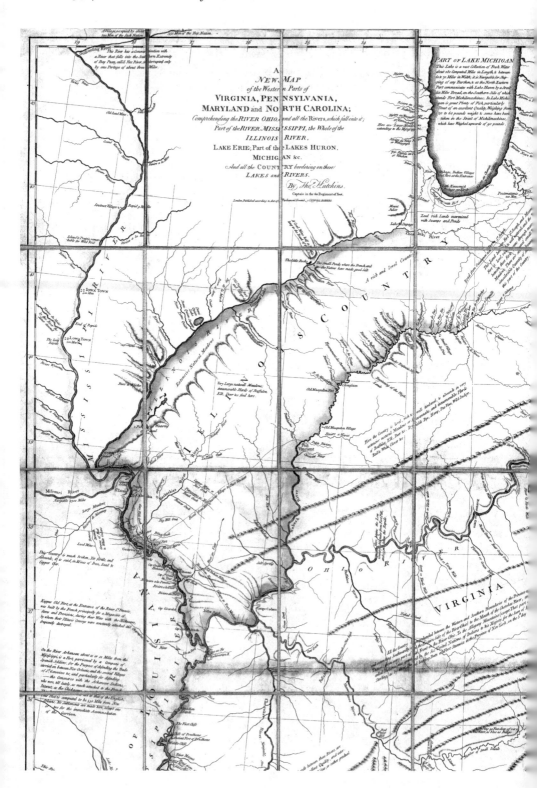

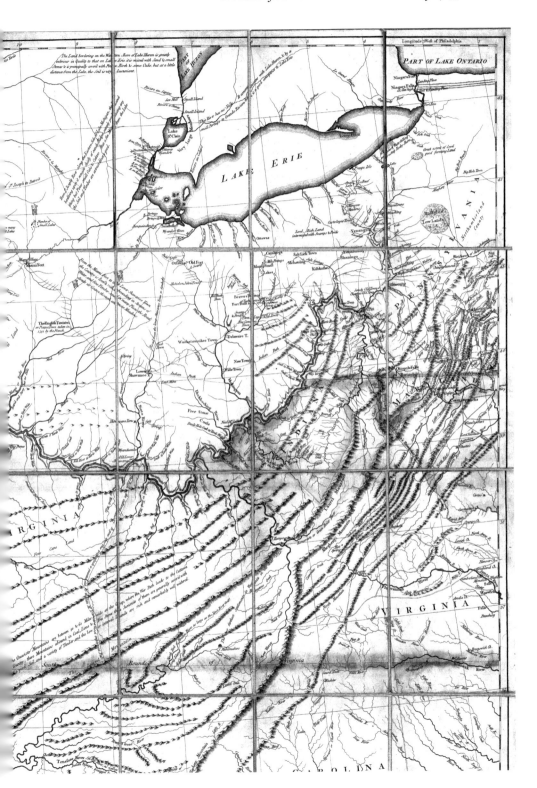

for relief. They wanted an Englishman to replace Rocheblave and argued no Englishman could remain in the region if he stayed.[16] For his part, Rocheblave corresponded with Lieutenant Governor Hamilton, blaming the English merchants for double-dealing and inviting Hamilton to send a subordinate to Kaskaskia to replace him, probably knowing that was unlikely.[17] (Of course, some of the English merchants were in fact, helping Americans seeking supplies from the Spanish.) The result was a divided and weakly led community. While Rocheblave and the English residents of Kaskaskia maneuvered politically against one another, Lord George Germain's letter unleashing an Indian war on the American frontier arrived in Hamilton's hands. Even if the lieutenant governor had been inclined to sort matters out in Illinois, he had more important issues before him. British authorities would continue to view the Illinois Country as a strategic backwater. Meanwhile, George Rogers Clark's spies, Benjamin Linn and Sam Moore, were already in town taking the pulse of Kaskaskia's residents and the local Indians.

CHAPTER FIVE

Clark Advances

May 12, 1778 to July 4, 1778

*W*hen Clark set out from the Monongahela on May 12, 1778, his 150 or so men were a surly lot. Significantly fewer than he had estimated necessary, Clark and his recruiters had struggled to assemble even that contingent. Clark's forces constituted three companies, joined by some families and various others seeking to establish new lives on the Ohio frontier or simply headed downriver.[1] It was customary for groups of people to travel the Ohio River in ad hoc convoys for security. Despite the added bodies, Clark still made swift passage to Pittsburgh and then down the Ohio. When Clark and his men reached the mouth of the Kanawha River, the commander of Fort Randolph there invited them to join with the garrison in pursuit of a large Indian raiding party headed for Virginia's Greenbrier region. Clark declined, fearing that the loss of time and potential for desertion would frustrate his designs in Illinois.[2]

To defend Kentucky from cross-river raids, the confluence of the Ohio and Kentucky Rivers was a logical place to build a fort. It was a critical point, as the latter wound to the heart of the new settlements. Clark's convoy stopped there, but the shortage of men prevented him from establishing and fortifying a post. Governor Henry had asked him to build a fort at the junction of the Ohio and Mississippi and the mouth of the Kentucky River was too far east to support his forces in Illinois. Although he did not mention it, any men stationed at the Kentucky River would also have an easy time deserting, either back up the Ohio or to the Kentucky settlements themselves. Clark decided he needed a post farther west, not primarily to defend Kentucky, but to help secure Illinois.[3] It was a risky call since the people of Kentucky and his soldiers were all under the impression Clark's force was there to protect Kentucky.

Clark already had an option in mind. Generally, the Ohio River flows rather slowly. At one point, however, it passed over a rough jumble of boulders, dropping some twenty-six feet over a two-mile run.[4] While not quite a waterfall, the rapids produced enough white water to appear so, giving the location its popular moniker, the "Falls of the Ohio." Today, the area is bound by parks in Indiana and Kentucky, although flood control measures have changed its geography and appearance. A garrison there would be far enough forward to support an invasion of Illinois and would help secure navigation of the Ohio since river vessels had to stop there to navigate passage.

Fortunately for Clark, the river boasted an island above the falls. Suddenly, the people who had accompanied him might prove useful. They could occupy the island in relative security, aided by the moat of the river and a small blockhouse. At seventy acres, it was large enough to plant some modest crops and gardens. Clark settled in on May 27.[5] Thus, the small, low-lying island became "Corn Island." After Clark proceeded to Illinois, the community there grew and moved to the southern bank of the Ohio, eventually becoming the city of Louisville.[6] (Corn Island was subsequently quarried into oblivion and no longer exists.) While Clark was at Corn Island, the Kentucky County lieutenant, Colonel John Bowman, brought in a few men, including only one of the four companies Major Smith had been expected to raise.[7] The other companies had dispersed in pursuit of raiding parties or were making up for security shortfalls exacerbated, in part, by the capture of Boone's party at the Salt Licks.

Clark, Colonel Bowman, and the officers conferred. They were much weaker than anticipated, while the British and Indians continued to expand their numbers, emboldened by the American frontier's weak defenses. Clark could not take every man available lest he leave Kentucky defenseless. Yet neither did he want to disband his tiny army to bolster the county's defenses, realizing that ceding the initiative to the British was a losing proposition. So, Clark and Bowman agreed their best course of action was to continue the offensive. Simply, they thought "it was better to Run a great Risque with one party than to divide our forces in such a manner as to Hazard the loss of boath."[8] While Clark was circumspect over the unfolding of that decision, the persuasive and charismatic abilities he had demonstrated at Harrodsburg and Williamsburg likely came into play.

Corn Island's isolation made it a good place for Clark to inform his soldiers of their destination and mission. Bluntly, it would be harder for them to desert. So, with an "army" smaller than a battalion of Continentals, he broke the news to his officers and soldiers. They were not there just to protect Kentucky but were bound for the Mississippi to invade the Illinois Country.

The reaction was mixed. The "Gentn warmly Espoused the Enterprise and plainly saw the utility of it, and supposed they saw the salvation of Kentucky almost in their Reach bit surely Repined that we ware not strong enough to put it beyond all doubt."[9] Clark's charisma carried the day with his officers; the soldiers were another matter and debated the issue, concluding that even success would leave them isolated and exposed without the possibility of reinforcements from Virginia. In short, they would be vulnerable. Should things go badly, a retreat might well be impossible. Someone raised the possibility of retreating across the Mississippi to sanctuary in Spanish territory. That seemed to settle the matter and most of the men decided to follow their officers, but members of one company remained disgruntled. Clark posted a strong picket on the boats to prevent anyone from deserting.

That night, Lieutenant Thomas Hutchins and the better part of a company swam and waded a small channel to the southern shore of the Ohio, deserting to Kentucky.[10] Clark had to admit he had been outgeneraled by a lieutenant. He formed a fast party, partially mounted on officer's horses, and sent it in pursuit with orders to execute every man who did not surrender. For their part, Hutchins' men had scattered, and Clark's pursuit party only caught a handful twenty miles away. Some of the deserters disappeared altogether, while others made their way to various settlements in Kentucky, where they apparently were taunted for cowardice.[11]

The desertion prompted Clark to improve discipline, largely to bend the men to his will by accepting the orders of their superiors. Drills were always a part of that process. Clark had already revealed his charisma; now he also began to demonstrate the hardness that would prove critical to his success. The lieutenant colonel was cryptically laconic describing what that meant, other than to indicate the returning deserters were welcomed by the effigy of Lieutenant Hutchins being hanged and burned. The deserters themselves were likely whipped and broken up among his various companies.[12] That the debate and desertion occurred, and Clark felt compelled to discuss it at some length in his memoir, indicates the lieutenant colonel's command authority was more tenuous than one might expect and highlights the extreme riskiness of his mission. It might just as easily collapse from within as from defeat by the British. He could not simply issue orders and expect men to follow due to his rank; he would have to lead. The challenges of keeping his men together highlight the heavy burden riding on the young commander's shoulders.

Improving discipline was necessary but did not require cruelty. Clark and his officers broke open a keg of rum to distribute among the men before they departed Corn Island on June 24.[13] Clark decided that most of Bowman's reinforcements needed to remain in Kentucky. He also left various families, adventurers, and a few soldiers behind on Corn Island under the command of Lieutenant Linn. So, the army bound for the Mississippi had only grown to 175 men, well short of the five hundred Clark thought he needed, or the 350 Virginia had authorized. The lieutenant colonel divided this group into four companies under Captains John Montgomery, Joseph Bowman, Leonard Helm, and James Harrod.[14] Clark's small force did not head directly for the falls but ran up the river about a mile to find the right channel. With that, they shot the rapids during a solar eclipse.[15]

Speed was critical and Clark was determined to move quickly. Rowing day and night with the oars double-manned, Clark's militiamen reached the mouth of the Tennessee River on June 28 and made camp on a nearby island. Within hours, they encountered a small hunting party, which Clark's troops brought into the camp. They were happy to share the latest intelligence.

The hunters explained that the Kaskaskia militia was well-ordered and expected to keep an eye out for Americans, but they also believed it was more for show and confirmed the 1777 intelligence that nobody expected rebels in the area. They also noted that the locals—Indians, French, and English alike—feared the Americans, particularly Virginians, having been convinced they were barbarous. Surprise was a distinct possibility, and the fear might play into Clark's hands. He could use that to intimidate the locals into submission, provided he could surprise them. After taking control, he could also demonstrate the kind of civility and forbearance that might even lead the local population to prefer its new American occupiers over the distant British officials.

Clark welcomed the information as he had heard little about the American Bottom since the year before. In particular "no part of their information pleased me more than that of the Inhabitants Viewing of us as more savage than their Neighbours the Indians, I was determined to improve upon this if I was fortunate enough to get them into my possession, as I conceived the greater the Shock I could give them at first the more sensibly would they feel my lenity and become more valuable friends; this I conceived to be agreeable to Human nature, as I had observed it in many Instances."[16] Better still, the hunters offered to guide the Virginians to Kaskaskia.[17]

Clark aimed his flotilla at Fort Massac, an abandoned French fort on the Ohio also known as Cherokee Fort and concealed the boats in a little creek above it. Rather than rowing up the heavily traveled Mississippi, the Virginians would march overland along game trails and through the wilderness. One local recalled, "The country between Fort Massac and Kaskaskia . . . was a wilderness of one hundred and twenty miles and contained, much of it a swampy and difficult road."[18] Across this rugged terrain, men had to carry their own supplies, including four days' worth of provisions. Rain held off, which lowered creeks and dried up water holes. Game became sparse and the men grew hungry. Morale suffered as anxieties over food and their vulnerability grew. Then the guide, John Saunders, got lost. Clark later wrote George Mason, "It put the whole Troops in the greatest Confusion. I never in my life felt such a flow of Rage—to be wandering in a Country where every Nation of Indians could raise three, or four times our Number and a certain loss of our enterprise by the Enemie's getting timely notice."[19] The Virginians decided Saunders was a traitor and had purposely misled them, but Clark was not convinced. He questioned the wayward guide extensively and conceded that the nature of the region lent itself to easy disorientation. Perhaps trying to buy time against precipitous action by his men, or perhaps to intimidate a possible traitor, Clark threatened to have Saunders executed if he did not quickly find a hunting trail that led east from Kaskaskia.[20] After an hour or two, the scout found a familiar location, got his bearings, and eventually led them within a few miles of Kaskaskia by the evening of July 4, six days after they set out.[21]

CHAPTER SIX

Kaskaskia Falls

July 4, 1778

*W*hile *Clark gathered his forces* and advanced down the Ohio, Hamilton felt confident that the war was going his way in the West. Events on the Upper Ohio River and in Kentucky boded well for the future. During the spring of 1778, Indian raiding constantly brought in prisoners, evidence of their success in destabilizing the frontier. The capture of Daniel Boone's work party in Kentucky was a particular coup. Hamilton reported to Governor Carleton that Boone claimed "the People on the frontiers have been so incessantly harassed by the parties of Indians, they have not been able to sow grain, & at Kentucke will not have a morsel of bread by the middle of June—Cloathing is not to be had, nor do they expect relief from the Congress."[1] In March, Hamilton received a wampum belt from the Iroquois Confederacy addressed to the Lake and Western Indian nations reminding them that the Six Nations had joined the British and encouraging them to do likewise and attack American settlements all across the region.[2] Hamilton's proclamation had reached the frontier, including the hands of the congressional Indian agent, George Morgan, at Pittsburgh. Four prominent frontiersmen—Alexander McKee, Matthew Elliott, and James and Simon Girty—fled Pittsburgh for Detroit. McKee had been an Indian agent for the British and had extensive contacts all along the frontier, while the Girtys had fought for the Americans.[3] (They also had extensive relations among Native American nations in the West.) In Western Pennsylvania and Virginia, their defection was viewed as bitterly as Benedict Arnold's was two years later. For Hamilton, it was a godsend.

Yet there were signs along the Mississippi that Britain's hold on the West was weaker than it appeared. Willing's mission had caused a panic in the Illinois Country, particularly in Philippe de Rocheblave's mind. Although Willing's orders took him south to New Orleans, he could just as easily have turned north and moved upstream against the Illinois Country, raiding towns along the American Bottom and Illinois River while seeking refuge and supplies in St. Louis on the Spanish side of the Mississippi. Then, he still would have been in a position to descend the Mississippi to New Orleans and threaten British settlements along the way, creating a more dire threat to the British in the West over a longer period. The failure of Willing's sponsors, the Continental Congress, the government of Virginia, and George Rogers Clark to coordinate their operations represented a missed opportunity. But they had different goals. Technically, Willing was supposed to secure supplies at New Orleans and return them to Pittsburgh, despite his pursuit of operations that resembled privateering more than securing war material for the war in the East. Virginia, of course wanted to secure its position in Kentucky and supply routes to New Orleans. Clark sought to defend Kentucky against Native American raids and create a threat to Detroit and Britain's Native American allies. Integrating all three goals was possible but beyond diverging political authorities.

Rocheblave shared some of Clark's views about the strategic importance of the Illinois Country. Having his own issues with Major General Carleton, largely over finances, the former French-officer-turned-Spanish-official-turned-British-commandant of Kaskaskia wrote directly to Lord George Germain in Britain to express his concerns:

[I] think there is but little known in regard to this country. It will soon become the center of communication between the Colonists and the Spaniards by means of the Mississippi and the beautiful river, which offers them connection with the Gulf Of Mexico and New Orleans. I have in vain set forth the danger of this, but have been powerless to prevent it from lack of means. I take the liberty my Lord of representing to you that the only means of saving this country and to guard against the numberless impediments to communication, is the immediate residence here of a lieutenant governor and troops.[4]

Indeed, all spring Rocheblave continued to warn about security and pleaded for more troops in the Illinois Country, alternatively attributing the need to Spanish machinations, Indian unreliability, wavering loyalties among the local population, the threat of American invasion, or some combination of all those factors. His concerns highlighted the social and political splits among the various identity groups that constituted the population of the Illinois Country. By July, as Clark's troops approached, Rocheblave was in a near panic, blaming the local citizens, particularly the local Englishmen, for the insecurity of the Illinois Country:

> Reckless spirits for the most part, they thought that the government owed them everything and that they owed nothing to the government. They raise a cry for liberty in all that concerns them, while their minds and hearts are full of schemes and oppression for all that does not pertain to themselves. . . . I beg you to see, sir, only an excess of zeal in the urgent solicitations I have the honor to make to you to send at once a body of troops here, to prevent the importation of an immense quantity of all sorts of aid for the colonies. All the alarms I have sought to give will be only too well realized. We are upon the eve of seeing here a numerous band of brigands who will establish a chain of communication which will not be easy to break, once formed.[5]

Rocheblave dated the missive July 4, not knowing how right he was. The pleas fell on deaf ears. Hamilton was confident that the Virginians could not mount a serious offensive. Instead, he was planning his own against Pittsburgh.[6]

Clark's force arrived outside Kaskaskia on the opposite bank of the Kaskaskia River a few hours before dusk, as Rocheblave was returning to Kaskaskia after dining with a Spanish official on the western bank of the Mississippi. The American settled his men in the woods and sent a few scouts forward to reconnoiter the town. After dusk, he picked up the march again, eventually occupying a house on the Kaskaskia River about three-quarters of a mile upstream from the town. His scouts reported that the Indians had largely departed, a high priority since they could quickly tip the balance in any battle. While there were a large number of men about, things were generally quiet.

Clark and his men occupied a home that held a large family successful enough to own several boats, which the Virginians commandeered to ferry themselves across the Kaskaskia River in the darkness. Although the home's residents were unclear and inconsistent about events in town and Clark heard a slight disturbance from the town's direction, he was "convinced that it was Impossible that the Inhabitants could make any resistance as they could not now possibly get notice of us time enough to make much resistance."[7] He had surprise on his side.

Clark split his little army into divisions with three missions: He would lead one party to the optimistically named Fort Gage while the others occupied the outskirts and interior of town in the dead of night. His men on the outskirts would prevent people from leaving and seize anyone approaching Kaskaskia. Those in the interior would patrol the streets and confine everyone to their homes.

In the darkness, Clark led his small party to the fort and seized Rocheblave in his bedclothes. With that, Clark's detachment offered up a general shout letting the rest of his men know they had seized the local commandant. The other detachments immediately began patrolling the town's streets and outskirts to ensure nobody left while those speaking French ran through the lanes and alleys declaring de facto martial law. They told the residents that anyone leaving their home would be shot "and in a very little time we had compleat possession and every Avenue guarded to prevent any escape to give the alarm to the other Villages in case of opposition."[8] There was a general ruckus among Kaskaskia's residents, but they eventually fell silent, no doubt intimidated by the racket the Americans made as they roamed the streets yelling warnings throughout the night, banging on doors, invading homes, and seizing any weapons they could find.[9] Within two hours, Kaskaskia had been seized and rendered defenseless without a hostile shot. The biggest town on the American Bottom was in American hands.

Back at Fort Gage, Rocheblave was generally uncooperative, demanding time to dress himself before departing his room and leaving his wife behind. Left unguarded, she took the opportunity to hide or destroy some of his important papers and likely any valuables.[10] Clark did not have her trunks searched. Throughout the remainder of the night, the lieutenant colonel had several residents brought before him for interrogation but learned very little.

When the sun rose, Clark faced a momentous task. He had seized the town, but he was deep in British territory and hundreds of miles away from the nearest American support. It was not enough to occupy Kaskaskia; he also needed to secure it, ensure the compliance of the bulk of the population, and transform it into a base of operations against the rest of the Illinois Country. Meanwhile, Vincennes lay to his rear. Troops there could readily descend the Wabash and cut him off from Corn Island and Kentucky, not to mention Pittsburgh.

Achieving his goals meant swaying Kaskaskia's population of about one thousand to his side, if not as outright supporters, then at least as passive residents.[11] (The town's population was split roughly down the middle between free and enslaved people.) For the town's citizens, Clark's presence also created an opportunity for the locals to upend the political order, get rid of the haughty Rocheblave, and settle some commercial rivalries and scores. Their eyes quickly fell on the richest man in the area, Gabriel Cerre, who was close to Rocheblave and coincidentally away from town. He was an extraordinarily successful trader and merchant, the chief competition of the Englishmen who had complained to British authorities about Rocheblave. They promptly accused Cerre of being a committed loyalist. Clark suspected something and moved quickly to secure Cerre's personal possessions and warehouses. Should Cerre be a committed loyalist, they could constitute the spoils of war. If he was inclined toward the Americans, there was no faster way to bring the influential merchant back to Kaskaskia.[12]

In the meantime, two locals professing to support the American cause provided a meal for Clark's men, who maintained their blockade. In town, Clark also restricted communications among residents while he sorted through village affairs. Comfortable that his troops had secured the town limits, he allowed the residents to move in and out of their houses and converse again. But he kept them in the dark about his own plans. In a bit of psychological warfare, Clark positioned himself as the mediator between the town's fears and his own goals; the citizens could look to him for their relief and protection from the dirty, armed, revolutionaries who had seized their town overnight. It was exactly how Clark wanted things.

As the citizens of Kaskaskia milled about and whispered among themselves, Clark peremptorily slapped a few militia leaders in irons. The town's leaders realized they needed to approach the Virginian to learn his purpose for being there and seek some sort of guarantees for themselves and their families. After all, they had been fed a steady diet of British propaganda about American barbarity. They settled on Father Pierre Gibault as their spokesperson.

Of all the people in Kaskaskia, Gibault was one of the most colorful. A Canadian-born Frenchman, he was ordained as a Catholic missionary in

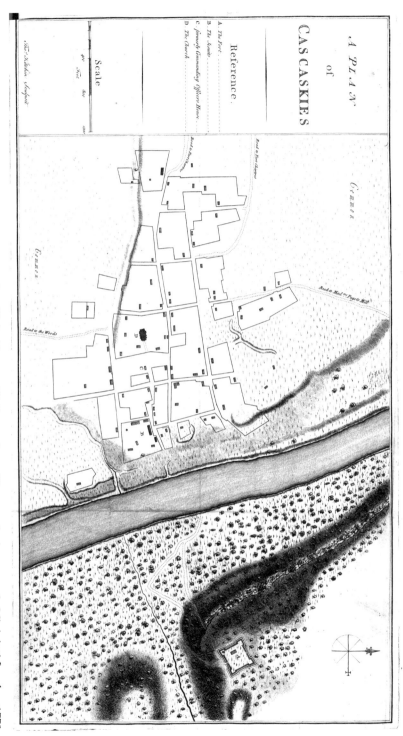

A PLAN
of
CASCASKIES

Reference.

A. *The Fort.*
B. *The .Asonic.*
C. *formerly Commanding Officers House.*
D. *The Church.*

Scale

Tho: Kitchin Sculpsit.

"A Plan of Cascaskies [Kaskaskia]," by Thomas Kitchin, from Philip Pittman, *The Present State of European Settlements on the Mississippi*, London, 1770. The old fort, labelled A, is across the river from the settlement.

1768 at thirty-one. His first assignment was the Illinois Country, where he made an odd appearance. Perhaps reflecting his prior experience on the frontier, he often went about wearing a brace of pistols, hunted, fished, played sports, and enjoyed the company of women. In short, he did not comport himself as a typical missionary. Gibault's behavior drew the attention, and condemnation, of his superiors, who frequently expressed concerns about the priest's mission.[13]

Perhaps it was Gibault's courage, his status as a priest, or his own initiative that made him the town spokesman. Whatever the circumstances, he and a group of older men received permission to meet with Clark and were eventually ushered into a building that Clark made his headquarters. Wrote Clark, "they ware shocked and it was some time before they would Venture to take seats and longer before they would speak."[14] Clark let the tension build before asking their purpose. Gibault spoke up. They feared being separated from their families and wanted time to meet in the church and bid one another goodbye. Clark, knowing the citizenry of Kaskaskia expected to be persecuted for their Catholic faith, casually gave them permission. But he would not grant them an extended audience. Clearly, the American commander meant to keep the town in a state of uncertainty and suspense, particularly on the topic of looting the town and breaking up families.

After a town meeting at the church, Gibault and the others approached Clark again. They thanked him for the indulgence of their church meeting and came quickly to the point: What was to be done with them? Before Clark could answer, they blamed their current situation on the war, Hamilton, their duty to obey British authorities, and general ignorance of the Americans or their reasons for making war on the Crown. Assuming their property was forfeit—perhaps based on precedent and Captain Willing's raid of the Lower Mississippi—they asked that their families be permitted to remain together with enough clothing and supplies to start over somewhere else. All things considered, it was a modest request, and one Clark was already more than inclined to grant. Indeed, with this demonstration of the town's submission, Clark knew he had achieved his psychological goal. For the American, "This was the point I wished to bring them to."[15]

It is tempting to dismiss Clark's narrative as so much after-the-fact boasting. But he shared an understanding of frontier warfare's nature with the French communities. It had long been brutal and made no distinctions between combatant and noncombatant. The assumptions and fears of Kaskaskia's population were entirely warranted, not just because British propaganda had frightened them into anticipating the worst from Virginians, but because the things they feared had happened time and again on the frontier. While those events might not have happened to French towns in the American Bottom in recent memory, they had happened to British frontier communities during the French and Indian War and Pontiac's War, with which the mixed communities along the Mississippi were all too familiar. One of the most famous instances of such a fate was the fall of Fort Granville on Pennsylvania's Juniata River in 1756, near the beginning of the French and Indian War. When word of an Indian war party in the area spread, local families gathered in Fort Granville to await developments and, hopefully, for the raiding party of Delaware Indians led by French officers to burn farms and depart the area. Instead, the war party laid siege to the fort. After negotiations, the defenders surrendered Fort Granville after being promised safe passage to Fort Duquesne. Instead, the inhabitants were deprived of their property and systematically tortured on the way to the Indian village of Kittanning. Some men escaped, but certain captives, including the wounded, were tortured to death or summarily killed. Survivors were transformed into de facto slaves of various tribes, which inevitably involved breaking up families. Among the most famous of these was the Girty family, whose defection to the British two decades later pleased Lieutenant Governor Hamilton.[16] Pennsylvania colonists retaliated by launching a raid against Kittanning, killing everyone they could catch and burning the village. Worse fates had befallen British families outside the walls and garrisons of forts all across the frontier during Pontiac's War in 1763. Massacres, the breaking up of families, and slavery were the currency of conflict on the American frontier.

Clark capitalized on that general fear. Whereas he tried to appear intimidating and indifferent to the fates of Kaskaskia's residents beforehand, Clark began to reveal his version of the generosity and fairness he hoped would bring the people of the Illinois Country to his side. He brusquely asked rhetorically whether they thought the Americans were savages, intent on making them go hungry while waging war on women, children, and the church. In other words, he played on latent racist fears and assumptions, revealing his own despite the fact that many of the French families were mixed.

Answering his own question, he blamed his presence in town on Hamilton's incitement of the Indians, denying that his forces had any intention of looting the town, distressing their families, or repressing the Catholic Church. Instead, he bragged that the United States embraced religious toleration and promised to defend Kaskaskia's citizens against attempts to interfere with their practice of their faith. After all, France and the United States were now allies. Clark announced they were free to conduct their affairs as usual and assured the populace that the British propaganda about American savagery was just that: propaganda. He pledged to let bygones be bygones and released those men he had clapped in irons just hours earlier, possibly with the intention of making this gesture. Property—including Kaskaskia's substantial enslaved population—would be held sacrosanct, although Cerre's property would remain under lock and key. All that was necessary was to comply with a proclamation he would shortly issue. With that, he dismissed Gibault and the gathered town leaders with instructions to spread the word throughout the town.[17] The Virginian's approach was distinctly different from James Willing's and it would show in the results. Kaskaskians expressed their relief with a celebration, ringing the church bells and thanking Clark profusely. Thus, Clark had captured the largest town in the American Bottom without a fight, and the residents were celebrating.

Seizing the Rest
of the
Illinois Country

July 5, 1778 to August 1, 1778

K*askaskia was in American hands,* but it was only the largest town in the American Bottom. Cahokia, Prairie du Rocher, and the old fort at Chartres on the Mississippi, as well as Vincennes and an old encampment named Ouiatenon by the French, with another abandoned fort on the Wabash, remained nominally under British control in the Illinois Country. To complete his conquest, Clark needed to capture those places as well, or at least ensure they did not become threats to his hold on the region. To that end, he loosened the cordon around Kaskaskia, believing that word of its capture and the kind treatment of its citizens would aid his campaign.[1]

With a population of nearly four hundred, Cahokia was the second largest town in the American Bottom and not far from the Spanish settlement at St. Louis across the Mississippi.[2] Clark hoped to seize it and cow it into switching sides much as he was doing in Kaskaskia. For that task, he selected Captain Joseph Bowman, whose brother John was the Kentucky

County lieutenant, to mount his company with horses from town and take it north, along with a few other men. He wanted Bowman to leave immediately, midday on July 5, but organizing the expedition took longer.[3] The delay was worthwhile.

Joseph Bowman was born in 1752, the eleventh of thirteen children of George Bowman and his wife, Mary Hite. The family moved to the Shenandoah Valley from Pennsylvania around 1731 and settled tracts of land in the lower valley south of Winchester. George owned a mill along Cedar Creek, just north of Massanutten Mountain and up to two thousand acres spread on the valley floor, which were worked by enslaved Black people. Shenandoah families provided a large percentage of males who served as militia to guard the colony's frontiers during the French and Indian War. In 1764, when Joseph was twelve, the nearby Miller family was murdered in their home a few miles away. One survivor, a daughter, arrived at George Bowman's door to report the attack that killed her parents and two siblings, which Joseph's older brother Abraham confirmed.[4] The same war party then attacked the Dellinger home, killed the father, and kidnapped his wife and baby. Pursuers, likely including Abraham, pursued the party and rescued the wife, Rachel. Her baby had already been killed. Those events illustrate the world in which Joseph Bowman lived his earlier years. By the late 1760s, two of Joseph Bowman's older brothers had relocated south and west in search of more land and 1775 found John Bowman visiting Kentucky, becoming a member of Harrodsburg's Committee of Safety in 1776.[5]

Joseph Bowman recorded his first will in 1773 and led a company in Dunmore's War against the Shawnee in 1774. His immediate postwar whereabouts are unknown, but as many of his extended relations were involved in exploring Kentucky as part of James Harrod's surveying mission, he likely participated. As a resident of Harrodsburg, he and his older brother John signed the June 1776 petition that Captains George Rogers Clark and John Gabriel Jones delivered to Williamsburg.[6] He had much in common with Clark: age, an extended family, ties to Virginia, travels in Kentucky, a financial interest in the frontier, some experience fighting Native Americans during Dunmore's War, and the kind of physical constitution that a hard life of successful hunting and exploration on the frontier demanded. Clark was placing his trust in a man much like himself.

As Bowman acquired his horses and prepared his men, word of his mission spread throughout town. Several residents of Kaskaskia offered to accompany him, arguing that he and his men were tired and the presence of

Kaskaskians would help achieve his goal. The residents of Cahokia were their friends and relations and such an open display of confidence in the citizens of Kaskaskia would have a salutary impact. Clark welcomed their presence: "I informed them that I made no doubt but that Majr Bowman would be fond of their company and that as many chose it might go."[7] Their logic was compelling, but Clark had the added security of their families remaining at Kaskaskia. With that, Clark added that the Kaskaskians should be armed for war: "[T]hese new Friends of ours was so Elated at the thought of the Perade they ware to make at Kohas that they ware too much Ingaged in Equ[i]ping themselves to appear to the best advantage."[8] This did not reflect a sudden conversion to the American cause, as events would prove. Rather, the locals sought to ingratiate themselves with the new power on the Mississippi and the expedition to Cahokia was an opportunity to protect family and business interests in the American Bottom.

Bowman's reinforced company did not leave until the night of July 5/6. In the dark, they swept up the small villages of Prairie Du Rocher and Saint Phillips on the way. Bowman recalled, the people "seemed scared almost out of their wits as it was impossible that they could know my strength."[9] Bowman and his men finally arrived at Cahokia late in the morning of July 6 and followed much the same process that led to Kaskaskia's fall: intercept people outside town who might warn of the American approach, move into the outskirts and infiltrate the town quickly to prevent anyone from entering, fleeing, or organizing a resistance, suddenly announce the American presence and occupation, intimidate the population into submission, and demonstrate a firm purpose, while also revealing an intention to govern graciously without harming or molesting the inhabitants. Clark described the action:

> [Bowman and his men] got into the borders of the Town before they were discovered the Inhabitants was at first much alarmed at being thus suddenly visited by strangers in a Hostile appearance and ordered to surrender the Town even by their Friends and Relations but as the confution among the Women and Children appeared greator than they expected from the cry of the big Knife being in Town they Amedeately assumed and gave the people a detail of what had happened at Kaskaskias the Majr informed them not to be alarmed that although Resistance at present was out of the question he would convince them that he would prever their friendship than otherways that he was authorised to inform them that they ware at Liberty to become Free americans as their Friends at Kaskaskias had or that he did not chuse it might move out of

the Cuntrey except those that had been ingaged in Inciting the Indians to war.[10]

The reaction was eventually the same: cheering, at least according to Clark.

It did not go exactly that way. When Bowman demanded the militia commandant take the oath of allegiance immediately, the man resisted. But, Bowman, still following the script of trying to bring the locals over to the American side, did not react. Warned that the commandant planned to collect some local Indians and counterattack, Bowman promptly arrested him and moved into a large stone house, which he fortified.[11] Then he and his men lay upon their arms the entire night, their third without sleep.[12] The next morning, Bowman required the locals to take an oath of allegiance to the United States or be treated as enemies. It is likely he and Clark had discussed the approach to take with Cahokia's residents. Before 10:00 a.m., 150 residents did, joined intermittently by another 150 locals over the succeeding ten days. It was enough for Bowman to feel reasonably secure. Nevertheless, he began repairing the fort, appointed a police force to maintain order, opened communications with the Spanish at St. Louis, and informed nearby villages and settlements that they were now free men living under the control of the United States. Freedom, of course, was not extended to Cahokia's enslaved population and the promise to respect property rights meant that slave owners need not fear the Americans as they had reason to fear Captain Willing earlier in the year. Willing had seized slaves on the spot and sold them in Spanish territory. Bowman's occupation was complete by July 8.

Clark now held the American Bottom, the key to the Illinois Country. But Vincennes on the Wabash, as large as Kaskaskia and closer to the Indian nations attacking Kentucky, technically remained under British control.[13] As he had in 1777, Clark sent spies into the region to scout out his next target. Simon Kenton, Shadrach Bond, and Elisha Batty traveled the 180 miles between Kaskaskia and Vincennes to assess the town and its defenses, a ramshackle timber stockade grandly named Fort Sackville after Lord George Germain, the Viscount Sackville. Donning blankets and posing as frontier traders, Kenton and his party ventured into the village and found that the British commandant, Captain Abbott, had departed. They returned the next day to maintain the deception that they were merchants. Then, Kenton and Batty went to Kentucky, in part to scrounge reinforcements, while Bond returned to Kaskaskia with the group's report.[14]

As Kenton's party performed its mission, Clark continued collecting information from the locals along the Mississippi and started preparing his own expedition to the Wabash. Although some Frenchmen from the American Bottom might join him, there was no denying his forces were already stretched thin and at the end of a tenuous supply line. If the paucity of forces available to him that summer had justified bypassing Vincennes, his problem had only grown worse with the need to defend his successes along the Mississippi.

Father Gibault rode to Clark's rescue. Vincennes was part of his charge and the Frenchmen there were part of his flock. He knew the region well and did not think a military campaign was necessary. "[H]e expected that when the Inhabitants was fully acquainted with what had past at the Illinois and the present happiness of their Friends and made fully acquainted with the nature of the war that their Sentiments would greatly change that he new that his appearance their would have great weight Eaven among the savages."[15] The priest believed that the residents of Vincennes would join the American cause if they understood Clark's purpose and how his forces had conducted themselves along the Mississippi. Indeed, he pledged to bring them over to Clark's side. Yet, because Gibault's role was spiritual, he could not be seen in such a political role. Instead, he preferred that Dr. Jean Baptiste Laffont lead a delegation to Vincennes, which would include Gibault.

Clark agreed, added his own spy to the delegation, provided Laffont with written instructions and "talking points" to use, gave Gibault verbal instructions about his expectations, and presented the group with a proclamation to be read to the people of Vincennes.[16] Even better, Laffont and Gibault were armed with correspondence for the residents of Vincennes from their relations in Kaskaskia, who could confirm their satisfactory treatment by the Americans. It was a reasonable risk for Clark to take for several reasons: He had few troops, despite the "reinforcements" of French militia who joined the American camp. (He did not confess this to anyone at Kaskaskia, preferring to let them believe American reinforcements were available to him at the Falls of the Ohio.) The English lieutenant governor had left. His own information about Vincennes indicated it was no bastion of loyalists. Rocheblave's correspondence with Carleton and Abbott's correspondence with Rocheblave, some of which Clark had access to, suggested that disloyalty was rampant in the Illinois Country, including Vincennes. The report from Bond's scouting mission was encouraging and Gibault had impressed him with his support for the American presence. Vincennes appeared ripe for exactly the kind of outcome the priest expected.

It took two or three days for the Frenchmen to reach Vincennes, where Gibault and Laffont went to work. Although Clark's personal skills were unavailable to them, the Virginian's talent for psychological warfare came in the form of his proclamation, which became the basis for Vincennes to change sides. In it, he explained that the American presence in the Illinois Country was the fault of the British, who had occasioned it by encouraging, supplying, and leading Native American war parties on raids across the frontier. He pointed specifically to Hamilton's June 1777 war councils. As a result, according to Clark, "The murders and assassinations of women and children and the depredations and ravages, which have been committed, cry for vengeance with a loud voice."[17] In other words, the Americans were out for blood, reason enough to fear them.

He then offered assistance and protection to the inhabitants of the Illinois Country while promising to treat them as citizens of Virginia—which he informed them the land they had lived on for generations as Frenchmen was—provided they swear an oath of fidelity to the state. Clark then raised what he thought was the best incentive: an offer to let them essentially govern themselves as Virginians. "If you accede to this offer, you will proceed to the nomination of a commandant by choice or election, who shall raise a company and take possession of the fort and of all the munitions of the king in the name of the United States of America for the Republic of Virginia and continue to defend the same until further orders."[18] The commandant would be commissioned as a captain; he and his men would draw rations and pay from the state of Virginia, which would also pay to improve any fortifications needed. A few left town but on July 20, 184 men signed the oath, which was taken at the church.[19] Gibault's party returned to Kaskaskia with the good news and a few men from Vincennes on August 1. Clark promptly dispatched Captain Leonard Helm and a few men to take charge and ensure that Vincennes remained in American hands.[20] With Helm's arrival, Clark had finished seizing the Illinois Country. Through masterful psychological warfare, achieved largely by employing surprise, intimidation, and incentives, Clark had displaced Britain without killing anyone. His next task was to secure and hold the Illinois Country as a defensive bulwark for Kentucky and Virginia's western borders. Native Americans were critical to that outcome.

CHAPTER EIGHT

Securing American Gains

August 1778 to September 1778

Even as he planned for Vincennes' capture, Clark had ample work to do along the Mississippi. Governor Henry gave him considerable latitude for the campaign after the capture of Kaskaskia. Clark decided to exploit it.

His public orders from Governor Henry limited enlistment terms to the time it took to reach Kentucky plus three months. Thus, Clark's battalion was about to evaporate, and he needed more men. That meant turning to the French, who had demonstrated some willingness to join the American cause. He had already made strides in that direction by encouraging them to form their own militia, subject to Virginia law, and appoint some of their own officers. But their reliability was questionable, and he still needed to lock down the French political structure to prevent his newly won control of the area from being undermined.

With that in mind, Clark's first order of business was resolving the issue of Gabriel Cerre, the wealthy and influential merchant who some residents of Kaskaskia accused of being a loyalist. The trader arrived in St. Louis from his travels in the Upper Great Lakes to find that his storehouses and other property in Kaskaskia had been seized and placed under lock and key by the new power on the Mississippi. Aware of the accusations against him, Cerre sent Clark a letter from St. Genevieve defending himself and offering to cross the river to discuss matters provided Clark would issue him a passport and permit him to depart.[1] Clark declined, insisting Cerre present himself without a promise of safe return. Surprisingly, perhaps, the merchant and trader did. Then Clark held a de facto trial, insisting that Cerre's accusers make their case. Whether their accusations fell apart in public or were weak to begin with, Clark pronounced Cerre innocent of the charges.[2]

In truth, the two were playing a high-risk game of chicken. Clark could not afford to alienate the merchant, whose wealth, trading networks, and influence with the Native Americans could make him a powerful opponent. For his part, Cerre had a prosperous business and wanted it to continue, not to mention recovering his goods at Kaskaskia. In that moment, it mattered little which flag flew from the fort. Loyalty, per se, whether to France, Spain, Britain, America, or a Native American nation was less important on the frontier than relationships and power among local groups. Despite Cerre's productive and profitable past with Hamilton and Rocheblave, the Frenchman and the Virginian both had a self-interest in working together. In pronouncing Cerre innocent, Clark also sent a signal to the French population that dominated the American Bottom: he respected them. It was a good message to send. No sooner had the Americans settled in along the Mississippi when various merchants began bombarding Clark to adjudicate their disputes with one another as well as matters left unresolved by Rocheblave. All he could do was try to address the easy ones and plead for unity and honorable behavior. Still, it was progress and helped solidify Clark's hold on local militia recruits of French descent.

Clark's success thus depended on French accommodation. They still constituted a majority of the white population and had largely been overlooked by British authorities. Indeed, early in the transition from French to British control—"control" being an ephemeral concept given the independence of Native American nations all across the region—British soldiers and merchants moving into the Illinois Country looked down on local French communities.[3] To complicate matters further, English trade on the Mississippi declined, hardly making it worth the expense of maintaining either a military or political commitment to the region.[4] In all likelihood, after 1763 at least some French traders simply moved across the Mississippi and continued their pre-British trade outside of the taxes and constraints of British rules. Clark may have simply offered a better deal. By proclaiming

Cerre's innocence, he essentially promised not to interfere with their trade. Rocheblave, French though he might be, had been officious toward both the French locals and the English traders and merchants who moved in after Pontiac's War. His influence seems to have come more from his semi-official position than his personality or strength of leadership. Clark was the polar opposite. In the moment, his influence derived from the barrels of the guns in his little army's hands and a cultivated reputation for ruthlessness. Over time, however, as the locals were allowed to rearm themselves, form a militia, and govern themselves within certain parameters, his charisma and intelligence became more important.

Clark's second order of business was to address the Native Americans in the region. After all, his original purpose in proposing the campaign was to relieve Kentucky from the British/Native American raids against it and begin separating Detroit from its Indian allies. Captain Helm had extensive relationships among the Native American nations in the Illinois Country and along the Wabash. He would take the lead from Vincennes while Clark remained on the Mississippi, calling a grand council of the local Indian nations to meet at Cahokia in August. Those attending included the Kaskaskia, Peoria, Winnebago, and Potawatomi. With the exception of the last nation, they generally had not been aggressive toward the Americans in the East. Smaller groups from the more militant Sauk, Fox, Kickapoo, Ottawa, and Ojibwe nations attended, more as observers than participants.[5] Indeed, the Algonquian-speaking Illinois Indians (Peoria, Piankeshaw, Wea, and Kaskaskia) and the French communities had been under military and economic pressure from the Sauk, Fox, and different clans of the Potawatomi for some time. Intertribal conflict may have done more to define the area than the British American war along the Atlantic coast, in part due to British neglect of the region.[6] With kinship and trade patterns more closely tied to the French, the fortunes of the Illinois Nations suffered as the French government withdrew from the area after the French and Indian War and the focus shifted from French New Orleans to British Pittsburgh. By some accounts, the Illinois Indians were already on the decline as a result.[7] In short, they lacked the wherewithal, and perhaps the desire, to participate alongside the British in the American Revolution. Indeed, they may have required from Clark the same protection from their enemies as he sought to obtain for the Virginians living in Kentucky!

Clark, not yet twenty-six years old, did not have long personal experience with Native Americans in the area and appears not to have understood the nuance among the various tribes he encountered. Instead, he lumped them all together, viewing them through the lens of Kentucky victimhood rather than appreciating the complex politics among Native American Nations along the Mississippi. Nevertheless, those complicated regional relationships created opportunities for Clark's brand of psychological warfare to pay dividends.

The Virginian had a different approach to Indian diplomacy and conducted his Cahokia council accordingly. Normally, when someone called a grand council, it involved large delegations making camp at the location and mingling, trading, drinking, and eating. Formal discussions opened with gift-giving as a sign of mutual respect and long speeches summarizing the speaker's view of the relationships among those gathered. (Gifts also served as incentives to go to war or bribes to maintain peace, although the relationship between gifts and behavior was decidedly more complex than that.) Such speeches were highly diplomatic, respectful, indirect, and, simply, time-consuming. Though in a hurry, Hamilton's June 1777 council had dragged on for days, even weeks for some participants. Clark disagreed with the approach in its entirety: "I had been always convincd to our Genl Conduct with the Indians was rong that Inviteing them to treaties was construed by them in a different manner to what we expected and imputed by them to fear and that given them great presents confirmed it. I Resolved to guard against this &c."[8] Instead, Clark would try to establish psychological dominance by striving to impress Indian attendees with his firmness and domineer them through barely veiled threats. George Rogers Clark's grand council would be no meeting of respectful equals.

After the usual opening ceremonies, the Native Americans spoke in turn, each blaming their roles in the war on the British and promising to cease raiding settlements and work for peace. It was good to hear. As was customary, Clark welcomed their words. For his part, Clark refused to offer customary greetings or signs of respect and promised to think overnight about what the Indians had told him.[9] He ominously committed to reply formally the next day, warning them that their continued existence as a people depended on what he concluded. Clark typically hid vulnerability with overt displays of overweening confidence. Just as he had used fear, uncertainty, and intimidation to seize the Illinois Country, Clark planned to use it to overawe the local Indian nations. With the Indians in town, Clark's meager forces were dramatically outnumbered. It was an extraordinary risk to take. He had few alternatives.

The next day, Clark was direct. First, he sought to build a rapport with the Native American community vis-à-vis the British by drawing comparisons between their situations. "The Big Knife are very much like the Red people they dont know well how to make Blanket powder cloath & c they buy from the English . . . and live chiefly by making corn Hunting and Trade as you and the French your Neig[h]bours do." He explained that the British restrained American trade and matters had escalated from there to the point where the English "should do as they pleased &c killed some of us to make the reast fear."[10] In Clark's telling, the Americans eventually rose up to fight. Clark's attempt to draw parallels only went so far, however. It was a patronizing attempt to explain the war to Native Americans in terms he thought they would understand; it was not an effort to place them on an equal footing.

Second, he blamed Indian participation in the war indirectly on American success against the British: "the English was drove from one place to another until they got weak and hired you the Red people to fight for them and help them The great Sperit getting angrey at this he caused your old Father the French King and other Great Nations to Joyn the Big knife and fight with them against all their Enemies . . . it is the great sperit that caused your waters to be Troubled because you Faught for the people that he was mad with and if your women and Children should Cry you must blame your selves for it and not the Big knife."[11] In drawing attention to the French king and France's new alliance with the Americans, Clark was tying the American presence to better days for Indians in the region, in contrast with the British. Like Hamilton, he was affording the Indians he addressed with agency in their own decisions, including responsibility over their past actions and autonomy in determining their future.

Third, Clark presented them with a clear choice, announcing "I am a man and a Warriour and not a councillor. I carry in my Right hand war and Peace in my left . . . to take possession of all the Towns that the English possess in this Cuntrey and to remain hear watching the Motions of the Red people" and stop those attacking the Americans. He explained the nature of the conflict between Great Britain and the Americans in terms he thought the Indians could relate to, but one that likely sounded condescending and overly simplistic. Native Americans were highly experienced with conflict among whites and had often leveraged it in their own conflicts among tribes. But it reveals something of Clark's attitude and his lack of nuance when it came to dealing with the local Indians. In any case, that may have helped the starkness of the choice he wanted to present: a sincere commitment to unrelenting war or peace. Clark continued his speech:

Hear is a Blody Belt and a white one take which you please behave like men and don't let your present situation being surrounded by the Big knife cause you to take up the one Belt with your hands when your Hearts Drink up the other If you take the Blody path you shall go from this Town in safety and Join your Freinds the English and we will try like Warriours who can put the most Stumbling Blocks in the Roads and keep our Cloaths the longest perfumed with Blood If you should take the Path of Peace and now be received as Brothers to the Big knife French &c and should hereafter listen to bad Birds that will be flying through your Land you will then be counted not men but having two Tongues ought to be destroyed without listning to what you say as nobody could understand you.[12]

In Clark's recollection, the next day the Indian leaders assembled, expressed their appreciation for his honesty, and chose peace. In Clark's mind, this confirmed his opinion of the proper way to negotiate with Native Americans, from a superior position, or at least the appearance of it. Clark often tried to create the impression that he represented a much larger force than he actually commanded; thus, the reference to surrounding the Native Americans at Cahokia. With that, "I had set a Resolution never to give them any thing that should have the appearance of Courting them but Genly made some excuse for the little I present[ed]."[13] In other words, he would not follow the French or British custom of gift-giving, which he viewed as bribery. In truth, stretched as thin as his own resources were, he had little to offer. Although Clark adjusted his negotiating tactics from tribe to tribe, his strategy did not differentiate among Native American nations, instead, lumping them all together as "Red Men." In his mind, he was securing peace with "the Indians." Unfortunately, at Cahokia it was with many of the wrong nations. Not all tribes agreed about their interests and goals in the American Revolution. Indeed, a Kaskaskia chief went to Ouiatenon after Clark's conference and sought to maintain a relationship with the British. In other words, despite Clark's attempt to present a binary choice, even the Indians most vulnerable to Clark sought to keep their options open.[14]

Nevertheless, Clark's approach was risky. If, instead of keeping their options open, the Native Americans had been as unified and committed to Britain as Clark thought, they could have quickly overwhelmed him and ended the Illinois campaign at that moment. Indeed, he was personally threatened at Cahokia. The Virginian made a point of living in a house outside the decrepit fort's walls, as if he did not fear the Indians. But he secretly filled it with armed men and kept a steady watch. Caution was warranted. Just after midnight one day, a group of Winnebago warriors rushed the house, claiming to seek refuge from an attack. A sentry spotted them approaching across a small creek, yelled an alarm, and alerted the Americans and French militia in town. Surprise lost, the Winnebago attackers scattered back to their camp. Clark and his men quickly descended on the Indian camps, heard rumors that the would-be attackers came from the Winnebago tribe, and identified them from their wet clothing. The Americans seized those who had waded the creek and slapped several Winnebago leaders in irons.[15] The next day, he proceeded with the council, saying nothing about the previous night's events. He wanted to create the impression that the Virginians were above such pettiness and that any Native American who would engage in such behavior was unworthy of his attention. In an attempt at reconciliation, some Winnebago leaders offered a peace pipe and belt in council; Clark's response was to stand and smash it with his sword, an outrageous response to such an offer. (It was not unprecedented. Hamilton did the same thing to efforts by the Delaware Indians to maintain peace in the Ohio Country.) Eventually, Indian leaders offered up two individuals for Clark to do with as he pleased as compensation for the event, which was different from actually offering them up as the guilty parties. Clark, of course, used the opportunity for a grand statement and pardon.[16] He was careful to include the local French and Spaniards in the process, demonstrating to them the value he placed on them and to the Indians that the French were on his side.

The Winnebago episode underscored Clark's all-or-nothing approach to diplomacy with the Native Americans. While individual Winnebago eventually accepted responsibility for the affair and begged forgiveness, which Clark granted, the Virginian's confrontational approach demonstrated the serious, and arguably ruthless, lengths to which he was prepared to go. Combined with his forgiveness of the Winnebago, it created the image of a terrible foe, but a reliable ally. Native Americans in the area might not be entirely convinced, but Clark's approach was a new one they had to consider.

Perhaps due to the starkness of the choice Clark attempted to create for Indians at Cahokia, it became the most famous episode in his diplomacy. It is even depicted on a twenty-eight by sixteen-foot mural inside the Clark Memorial at the George Rogers Clark National Historical Park in Vincennes, Indiana. It was not his only effort, however. Shortly after the Cahokia council, Clark received word that an Ojibwe chief named Blackbird wanted to meet with him. The feeling was mutual. Blackbird was influential among the Indian nations living along the St. Joseph River in today's Southwest Michigan. As the Ojibwe had closer ties to Britain, making inroads among them might do more to relieve pressure on the American frontier than making peace with the Illinois tribes. As Clark understood it, Blackbird was in St. Louis when Bowman seized Cahokia. Because the chief placed little confidence in Spanish protection from the Americans, he and his party quickly returned home to await events.[17] As much as Clark wanted to separate Britain from its Indian allies, Blackbird sought advantage for his people. Eventually, perhaps assured of their safety by Clark's release of the Winnebago Indians at Cahokia, the chief and eight men visited Clark at Kaskaskia.

Although Clark's disdain for Native Americans drips from the pages of his draft memoir, his retelling of their meeting rings true in its main points. Blackbird asked to dispense with traditional ceremonies and speak directly across a table, suggesting familiarity with how whites conducted business with one another (and why shouldn't he be) and got right to the point. Blackbird opened the meeting and told of a past desire to meet with leaders from the rebelling colonies because he was concerned the British were deceiving Native Americans on the frontier. Acutely aware that he had only heard a one-sided version of events, he wanted an American perspective and did not trust what he had been told by prisoners seized on the frontier. Clark patronizingly felt "obliged to begin almost at the first settlement of America and to go through almost the whol History of it to the present time particularly the cause of the Revolution and as I must not speak to him as I did to other Indians by Similes it took me near half a Day to satisfy him."[18] According to Clark, Blackbird offered to join the Americans and the French. The Virginian demurred, but simply asked the chief and his nation to sit out the remainder of the war. As some Ojibwe were already away from their villages on raids, Clark would have to excuse their activities until they returned to the area, when Blackbird would prevent those who he had influence with from continuing the war. Clark believed he had scored a major coup.

Blackbird's perspective may be more interesting, although appreciating it requires some speculation. Despite many American beliefs, Native Americans in the Great Lakes were not staunchly allied with the British. Indeed, even after victory in Pontiac's War and Dunmore's War, the British presence was tenuous. Traders in the region depended on forts, which depended on both the sufferance and supplies provided by Indians across the region.[19] Meanwhile, the Native American nations could continue trading with the

French and Spanish across the Mississippi, all the way down to New Orleans. Thus, to a degree, they could still play the British off against the French and their Spanish replacements.

For the St. Joseph Ojibwe and Odawa, part of a larger group of Native Americans known as the Anishinaabeg, war had been profitable. It had made them more valuable to the British, which the British understood, and they turned out to support British ambitions in Canada in 1776. By the spring of 1777, local British officials were raising expectations that the Anishinaabeg would turn out again as British allies. But few warriors traveled east to join Burgoyne during his unsuccessful campaign in New York. As the year progressed, the British supplied, supported, and rewarded successful raids while making promises of future protection. As the Odawa understood it, this was merely the fulfillment of promises made for eternal protection and support from British-controlled Montreal in the midst of Pontiac's War. However, Odawa trust of the British was conditional. A smallpox epidemic struck the Odawa shortly after a delegation visited Montreal. Many in the tribe concluded that it had been sent by the British due to the close relationship between the Odawa and French.[20] Anishinaabeg returning from Burgoyne's campaign expressed their frustration with the British.[21] The general limited their provisions, held them collectively responsible for excesses, and forced British officers upon raiding parties, which could be taken as an insult. Thus, Blackbird's suspicion of the British and his eagerness to understand the changing political dynamic in Illinois were natural. If the American presence meant a return of French influence in the area, as Clark implied, then Clark's occupation of the American Bottom might prove a welcome development. At a minimum, Clark was a new variable who would affect events nearby. (Tensions between tribes were brewing in the Upper Great Lakes and Blackbird had more important matters of war and peace in front of him than the American-British conflict). From Blackbird's perspective, there was no harm in giving Clark what he wanted, at least in the moment. For Clark, his new approach to Indian relations was paying dividends. In truth, his presence in the Illinois Country might well play into Indian hands and leaders like Blackbird viewed events through a different lens. Time would tell whose approach determined the relationship.

Clark's interactions with other tribes along the Wabash River also deserve attention. Just as the Ojibwe and the Odawa were belligerent toward the Americans, so were the Piankeshaw and Potawatomi. The Piankeshaw chief Grand Coete, also known as Old Tobacco among whites, led a large community on the Wabash and initially rejected Clark's peace overtures. But Old Tobacco eventually reversed course. He was using Clark in much the same way the French communities and Ojibwe did: to maneuver against other political players in the area. Old Tobacco had recently agreed to a land transfer with the Wabash Company against the reservations of other Piankeshaw leaders. Thus, for Old Tobacco, Clark's presence represented an opportunity to advance his agenda. In the moment, agreeing to peace with Clark was the best way for Old Tobacco to improve his position vis-à-vis other Piankeshaw chiefs.[22]

At the end of the day, Clark's diplomacy had mixed results, scoring its greatest successes among the Illinois nations, which were not an active threat to Kentucky. Farther away, in the Great Lakes and Ohio Country, where the British found their greatest support, Clark's diplomacy had less of an impact on the war in Kentucky. Instead, some of the Great Lakes tribes used the opportunity to extort more goods from the British.[23] For Kentucky, little changed. The most aggressive Indian nation raiding Kentucky was the Shawnee, who generally continued their attacks unaffected by Clark's presence in Illinois or his diplomacy. In September, Black Fish led another Shawnee raid into Kentucky, where he besieged Boonesborough for nearly two weeks. The Kentucky County lieutenant, Colonel John Bowman, wrote Clark in October, "The Indians have Done More Damige in the Interier Settlements this summer than was ever Done in one seasons before."[24] As of that fall, Clark's campaign had failed to achieve its strategic purpose. Still, the Virginian believed his diplomacy with the Native Americans had worked in a small measure; his scouts were able to travel unmolested throughout the Illinois Country.

Clark's third task was to set up a government and entrench Virginia's power in the Illinois Country. Military occupation was unsustainable and would undermine his goal of bringing the region over to the American side as useful participants. The benefits of his acceptance of the French social structure and trade relationships might not have lasting effects if he could not give the locals a regular means of governing themselves. To that end, he set up a court system and had the locals elect their own magistrates. Unsurprisingly, perhaps, the Americans won the elections. Captain Bowman became the magistrate at Cahokia, where he served as commandant.[25] At Kaskaskia, Clark served as the chief appellate judge. Helm would remain at Vincennes, where Clark hoped Virginia would send reinforcements.[26]

Clark's last order of business was to augment his forces and shore up his defense. His progress with the Native Americans and French notwithstanding, the ease with which they had exchanged their British inclinations or obligations for neutrality or status as Virginians did not inspire confidence in their reliability. Thus far in the campaign, his Virginians had been augmented by a trickle of messengers and scouts coming and going from the frontier. Still, he needed more Virginians and managed to convince one hundred of his men to reenlist for another eight months. The remaining seventy left on August 4 under the command of Captain Linn, bound for the Falls of the Ohio. Rocheblave, who was incorrigible in captivity, accompanied them as a prisoner, while Captain Montgomery joined the group, bound beyond the Appalachians to deliver Rocheblave to prison and report to Virginia's government.[27] Montgomery was also to request that Virginia send a county lieutenant or other officials who could take over the governance aspects of Clark's mission. Hopefully, he could also squeeze reinforcements out of the state government, while Linn scrounged them from Kentucky County. Clark established a separate company of French militia officered by Frenchmen. It was not sanctioned by Virginia's government, but Clark believed Henry's orders gave him sufficient latitude to take that step.

He also shifted his supply lines. While the Ohio River would remain vital, the Mississippi was more reliable and Clark began communicating with the congressional agent in Spanish New Orleans, Oliver Pollock. Pollock had already actively supported operations along the river, particularly Captain Willing's supply mission earlier that year. Willing's raids along the Lower Mississippi had made him something of a burden to both the Spanish and Pollock, but keeping the American supplied and disposing of his booty gave the agent greater reason to build and maintain a network of merchants, traders, and supply depots along the Mississippi between New Orleans and the American Bottom. He now put it to work on Clark's behalf, supplying clothing and ammunition. (The Ohio remained critical for men, food, and communications with the settlements in Kentucky and the Virginia government.)[28]

Clark made significant progress in all these activities throughout the summer and fall of 1778. In the course of his actions, he also maintained the firm appearance of strength and ruthlessness, inflating his numbers through deception, drilling his men continually to maintain the discipline that had brought the Americans thus far and bring the French militia up to his standards. He had augmented his numbers with locals, established American governance of the region, and made significant progress undermining British power in the Illinois Country. Kentucky was by no means safe, but Clark's position on the Mississippi gave the Americans another axis of advance against Detroit should they be able to use it. Having achieved such ambitious goals with the barest of resources, Clark was at something of a loss.

George Rogers Clark by James B. Longacre, c. 1830. Clark did not sit for a portrait in his youth, but artists still captured his broad features. (*National Portrait Gallery*)

Lt. Gov. Henry Hamilton. Hamilton was one of four lieutenant governors of Quebec during the Revolution and by far the most reviled by Americans on the frontier, who called him the "Hair Buyer." (*New York Public Library*)

Father Pierre Gibault. The colorful priest flirted with women and could often be seen carrying a brace of pistols during his travels. (*Indiana Historical Society*)

Francis Vigo. The frontier trader was born in Italy, served in the Spanish Army, worked with the French, and helped supply Clark's forces only to be captured by Hamilton's men. (*Author*)

Upper left, "Pacane Miamis Chief," Miami, upper right, "Wawiachton a Chief of Poutcowattamie," Potawatomi, lower left, "Old Baby Ouooquandarong," Wyandot, lower right, "A Jibboway Indian, Ojibwe. These extraordinary illustrations were sketched by British Lt. Gov. Henry Hamilton in late 1778/early 1779 in the Illinois Country, possibly at Vincennes. Hamilton's personal experiences with Native Americans did not begin as lieutenant governor. He had been a prisoner of the French and encountered Native Americans during the French and Indian War. (*Harvard University*)

Indian of the Nation of the Kaskaskia.

Indian of the Nation of the Shawanoes.

Left, "Indian of the Nation of the Kaskaskia." Right, "Indian of the Nation of the Shawanoes" [Shawnee]. These engravings were based on original sketches by Georges H.V. Collot from his 1796 travels along the Ohio and Mississipi Rivers, published posthumously in 1826 as *Voyage dans l'Amérique Septentrionale.* (*Library of Congress*)

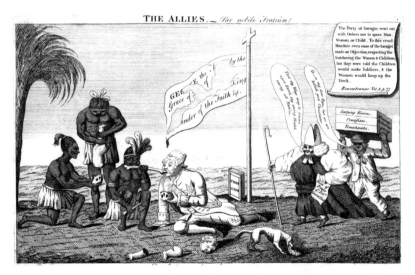

"The Allies—Par nobile Fratrum! [A noble pair of brothers!]" A political cartoon published in 1780 satirizing the claim in the Declaration of Independence that the king "endeavoured to bring on the inhabitants of our frontiers the merciless Indian savages." The image highlights white attitudes associating brutality with Native Americans while ignoring their motivation and interests and comparable behavior from whites. (*Library of Congress*)

"Shelb — ns sacrifice," 1783. Lord Shelburne watches American Indians slaughter loyalists, while Britannia with raised spear attacks him. Shelburne was prime minister in the final year of the American Revolution. Throughout the war, Britain's alliance with Native American nations was controversial in Britain, where many condemned it. (*Library of Congress*)

The Wabash River at Vincennes from the Indiana shoreline. (*Author*)

Ezra Winter painted seven murals that hang on the inside of the George Rogers Clark Memorial at George Rogers Clark National Historical Park in Vincennes. Four depict events in the Illinois campaign, including the council at Cahokia, crossing the Wabash River, the attack on Fort Sackville, and Henry Hamilton's surrender. Fort Sackville was less imposing than in Winter's painting. (*National Park Service*)

The George Rogers Clark Monument at the University of Virginia. Dedicated in 1921, the statue was removed from campus in 2021. (*Wikipedia/Smash the Iron Cage/CC4.0*)

George Rogers Clark Memorial at George Rogers Clark National Historical Park. The memorial sits on fill roughly where Fort Sackville stood. (*Dave Sterner*)

CHAPTER NINE

Hamilton's Counteroffensive

August 3, 1778 to October 27, 1778

O^{*n August 3, 1778*}, Rocheblave stopped tormenting his jailors long enough to steal away and write Governor Carleton a note. He informed the governor that he had been taken prisoner and a "self-styled" Colonel Clark had occupied Kaskaskia. He then proceeded with a litany of complaints and blame-assigning, all of which exempted himself of responsibility for the loss.[1] Hamilton received the letter in days and forwarded it, not knowing that Carleton had been replaced with General Sir Frederick Haldimand.

Hamilton dismissed Rocheblave's claim that three hundred men had occupied Kaskaskia. Instead, he assumed it was some portion of those who had joined Captain Willing on the Lower Mississippi earlier in the year. Everyone had anticipated that Willing would ascend the Mississippi to Kaskaskia, as indeed he had threatened to do. Hamilton's skepticism about the number of invaders was sensible, but for the wrong reasons, and he initially misunderstand American intentions. Willing was a raider who plundered English plantations and moved on. Clark was there to stay. The lieutenant governor dispatched a subordinate to the Wabash, both to solidify relationships with the Native American nations there and to prepare Fort Sackville at Vincennes for either defense or abandonment.[2] He suspected, accurately, that the Americans would quickly seize it as well and did not want the fort's war materiel to fall into their hands. Of course, the people in Vincennes had already switched sides and Captain Helm was sitting in Fort Sackville, which the Americans had renamed after Patrick Henry.

In truth, Rocheblave's complaint about Hamilton's inattention to the Mississippi had merit. The lieutenant governor, indeed, the entire British government, largely overlooked the Illinois Country during the American Revolution. Hamilton focused his strategic aims on the Virginia and Pennsylvania frontiers. While Clark and his battalion made their way down the Ohio and then marched toward Kaskaskia, Hamilton gathered multiple Indian tribes at Detroit for a grand council. He applauded their success after the 1777 council, declaring,

> you know the consequences have been good as you have succeeded in almost all your enterprises, having taken a number of Prisoners, and a far greater number of Scalps. You have driven the Rebels to a great distance from your hunting grounds . . . and you have forced them from the Frontiers to the coast where they have fallen into the hands of the King's Troops. . . . I have the pleasure to inform you that some of your younger brothers are desirous of having an Axe delivered to them, to use against your enemies who have rebell'd against the King.[3]

Indeed, the number of Native American nations willing to join the war against the Americans had grown, and with them Hamilton's ambitions.[4] McKee and the Girty brothers had filled him in about political divisions and military weaknesses at Pittsburgh, which might be ripe for a large-scale Indian raid, larger even than the ones aimed at the Kentucky settlements or Fort Henry the previous year.

Although he was often described as *the* lieutenant governor of Quebec, Henry Hamilton was only one of four lieutenant governors of Quebec in the American interior. Given the province's size, the full governor needed several lieutenants scattered among several critical locations to manage British affairs. Edward Abbott at Vincennes, who had questioned Britain's Indian policy, was gone before Clark began his campaign. Major Arent Schuyler DePeyster, a New York loyalist, held the position at Michilimackinac. The lieutenant governor appointed for Kaskaskia never assumed his post and Captain Hugh Lord performed the duties in his stead until appointing Rocheblave as his replacement when Lord left the area.[5] Nevertheless, given Detroit's size and centrality, Hamilton became the de facto senior lieutenant governor reporting to the Quebec governor and tended to think in broader terms than his compatriots.

Hamilton came from a line of second and third sons in the Scottish aristocracy. He was educated, but his prospects for noble titles were slim. Government service was a viable alternative for advancement, and he joined the Fifteenth Regiment of Foot at the age of twenty-one. Hamilton served in the colonies during the French and Indian War and gained his first exposure to Native Americans during the Canadian campaigns. Wounded and later captured by the French, Hamilton noted a feeling of discomfort on the frontier: "Shortly after this we prisoners were marched ostentatiously thro' the Indian encampment, where I saw not without a very unpleasant feeling, the Savages employed some in scraping and dressing Englishmens Scalps, others in whetting their Knives and Tomahawks."[6] Hamilton was no stranger to frontier brutality.

After the war, the future lieutenant governor at Detroit continued in government service, making his way up through the ranks of the British Army, until he sold his commission in 1775. In retrospect, it was poor timing and his lack of military rank complicated relations with military officers still in Detroit and elsewhere, not to mention his superior, Governor Carleton.

When word of Clark's success in the summer of 1778 arrived, Hamilton and the British changed plans. Attention shifted from the Pennsylvania and Virginia frontiers to the Mississippi River. Reading the news from the Illinois Country, Governor Haldimand directed Hamilton to develop a plan to recover the region using the resources he had already gathered for the campaigning season.[7] Ideally, Hamilton would destroy Clark's force, which represented the bulk of the American military power on the Lower Ohio River, encourage more Native American nations to join the British side, and still be free to conduct a campaign against Pittsburgh by the spring of 1779. At worst, he would isolate Cark in 1778 and finish the Americans in 1779. The possibility of abject failure seemed never to have entered British calculations.

Hamilton quickly surveyed the forces available to him at Detroit. The King's 8th Regiment was stationed in Quebec scattered across several posts, including Quebec, Michilimackinac, Fort Joseph (established on the St. Joseph River near Blackbird's Ojibwe), Fort Niagara, and Detroit. Because he had resigned his military commission, he could not plausibly order Captain Richard Lernoult of the army contingent at Detroit to provide troops for an expedition to counter Clark in the Illinois Country. Indeed, Lernoult and Hamilton had already clashed over their respective lines of authority in Detroit and the best courses of action in their area.[8] In the event, Detroit was undergarrisoned as it was and Lernoult only provided a lieutenant, two sergeants, and thirty men. Hamilton had to turn to other military resources. There were six companies of local militia, including a large number of Frenchmen. A handful failed to muster or declined to serve on the campaign. Hamilton looked for fresh volunteers and disarmed the "disaffected," requiring them to assist in mobilizing resources for the campaign.[9] He scraped together three officers, two sergeants, and around seventy rank and file from that conglomeration and a like number of white "volunteers," who were not mustered through the militia, but had apparently trained together. Roughly sixty Indians in the immediate environs also agreed to join the campaign. Altogether, it was about 240 men.[10] To recover such a large area, and still unsure of what he faced, Hamilton would need a larger army. Naturally, as he had done before, he turned to the Native Americans.

Leaders, warriors, and families from several prominent nations were still in the Detroit area from the grand council that Hamilton had convened that summer. On August 23, some Odawa, Ojibwe, and Potawatomi clans held a council and pledged to join Hamilton on his march to Illinois. Wyandot leaders joined the council and made similar promises the next day. White volunteers from the local militia mustered and Hamilton divided them into two detachments. Still, it was a small force. He would have to gather more Indians along the way. That meant reassembling the Odawa, Ojibwe, and Potawatomi warriors who had drifted away from Detroit before word arrived of Clark's success. More importantly, perhaps, he wanted to collect forces from the Miami, Wabash, and Scioto River basins, and smaller nations that he would encounter on his march to Vincennes and, eventually, the Mississippi. Clark was already working to split those tribes from the British.

Collecting allies for a specific campaign meant supplying them and ample gift-giving. To that end he divided his forces into two bodies. Captain Normand MacLeod would command a supply column, follow the Detroit River to Lake Erie, cross to the mouth of the Maumee River near today's Toledo, ascend the river to a portage and then to a tributary of the Wabash near today's Fort Wayne, and then be in a position to descend the Wabash with Hamilton's main army when it arrived. Along the way,

MacLeod was to establish supply caches, build roads, conduct diplomacy with the local Indians, and pave the way for Hamilton's main force. The Miami nation had one of its collections of villages near the portage, so he had to make a good impression. Thus, a large portion of MacLeod's supplies were destined for that area, collectively referred to by whites at the time as "Miami Town."

While Hamilton dashed off letters to British officials at Quebec and Niagara, sent envoys to various Indian nations, trained his militiamen, assembled boats, and collected supplies, MacLeod did the same, but on a smaller scale and with more urgency. Before Hamilton could start for Vincennes, the captain's expedition needed to be well on its way. Finally, as the leaves began to fall and dropping temperatures heralded the approach of autumn, MacLeod set out in approximately fifteen pirogues with roughly fifty militiamen, five pair of oxen, ten horses, three sets of wheels, and thirty-three thousand pounds of supplies.[11] "Pirogue" is a generic term referring to a canoe-like boat suitable for river traffic. Pirogues could be quite large, carry a few tons of supplies, and were often rowed rather than paddled. MacLeod's had to be large enough to carry livestock and withstand the potentially rough waters of Lake Erie, while remaining manageable by small crews in the narrow rivers around Miami Town.

The Revolutionary War frontier was filled with colorful characters, from the relentless and charismatic George Rogers Clark and the gun-toting, flirtatious priest Pierre Gibault to the officious chameleon Philippe de Rocheblave and the flashy lieutenant governor, Henry Hamilton. Alas, Normand MacLeod was not one of them. Instead, he played his part with phlegmatic competence, the kind of soldier who takes on the difficult work and does it well, who might not get the credit for great things, but without whom great things could not be done. So, it was natural for Hamilton to turn to the Scotsman for the difficult labors of paving the way to reach Vincennes over rough terrain in what promised to be worsening weather.

Born on the Isle of Skye, probably around 1731, MacLeod served in the British Army from at least 1747 to 1764 with the 42nd Highlanders—the famed Black Watch—in Holland, Belgium, and North America. Likely with the regiment when it was decimated attacking Fort Carillon, MacLeod later transferred to the 80th Regiment, Gage's light infantry, and made captain in 1760. During this time, he first visited Detroit and encountered Sir William Johnson, Britain's most renowned Indian agent and the man who figured prominently in determining the course of MacLeod's postarmy future.

With cutbacks after Pontiac's War in 1763, MacLeod went on half pay and began a career in Indian affairs as Johnson's representative, agent, and commissary, holding various posts in New York and Canada, frequently relocating. For many British officials on the frontier, it was a path to some wealth and influence, but not for MacLeod, who continually suffered from financial problems and eventually gave up. Instead, he cashed in on British promises of land grants to British veterans and tried farming in New York's Mohawk Valley while noticing the growing colonial dissatisfaction with British governance. A good soldier, he maintained a proper disdain for Americans, even though he was on the road to becoming one. Sometime in 1774, he gave up on New York and moved his family to Detroit, joining a partnership as an Indian trader. By the time the American Revolution was being waged in earnest, Hamilton had appointed MacLeod as Detroit's town major, essentially the chief executive officer for Detroit's militia-based garrison, from which he drew his pay.[12] His army rank remained captain and it was in that capacity that Hamilton put him in charge of leading an advance party on the route to Vincennes.

When George Rogers Clark set out from his rendezvous point at Redstone in May, he faced a relatively smooth passage (except for the Falls of the Ohio) and cooperative weather all the way to the Mississippi. His choice to approach Kaskaskia overland was tactical, hoping to give him the element of surprise. MacLeod was not so fortunate. Leaving Detroit at the end of September, autumn in the Great Lakes was already approaching. With shallow hulls and a low freeboard, pirogues were ill-suited to dealing with the waves that could kick up on Lake Erie in difficult weather, even skirting the coastline. Constant rain and wind slowed MacLeod's progress all the way to the Maumee, and his small flotilla frequently sought shelter in coves and bays that dotted the lake's western shores. It rained so much that MacLeod and his men had to unload and load their flour frequently, sometimes nearly all 26,800 pounds of it, to ensure that it remained dry.

By October 5, he had only reached the foot of the Maumee's "Great rapits," probably in today's Grand Rapids, Ohio, southwest of Toledo.[13] His men chose that moment to make demands. Their flour ration had spoiled in the rain, and MacLeod had to issue flour from the stores intended for Hamilton's army and its Native American allies. Still, when MacLeod and his men were able to move, they made good time on the river. Despite fog, rain, and the need to bring cattle along with him, MacLeod described a relatively peaceful trip. For some days, the fish were so plentiful that they even jumped into the boats.[14] His primary obstacle remained weather that threatened his cargo.

Along the way, MacLeod encountered messengers and scouts that Hamilton had dispatched earlier to tell the Indian nations in the region that he was coming with an army and to ensure their loyalty, such as it was. They also reported a range of rumors, from the truth that Clark was largely settling in on the Wabash with a few men to the idea that he was advancing with a few hundred or nearly one thousand men. The British captain promptly received what intelligence was available and assisted those scouts in taking their news to Hamilton, preposterous as it sometimes was. On the afternoon of the eighth, MacLeod's convoy finally reached an Indian village known as "The Glaize" at the junction of the Maumee and Auglaize Rivers, where Defiance, Ohio, sits today. (The town takes its name from a fort General Anthony Wayne built there in 1794, during the Northwest Indian War.) MacLeod was just over halfway from the mouth of the Maumee to the portage.

Although the local Indians welcomed him, they had little to offer and instead sought MacLeod's reassurances that Hamilton was in fact coming. Word continued to trickle in from the Wabash that the Virginians had arrived in great numbers and might even at that moment be marching north, demanding that local Indian tribes declare themselves openly and choose war or peace. Clark's intimidation campaign was working. MacLeod's own men grew shakier still and he reported to Hamilton, "there News So Intimidated my Party that I am Sure ten men would take us all Prisoners."[15] Nevertheless, MacLeod continued his mission.

Weather forced the British to delay at the Auglaize, so MacLeod dispatched men to the portage, where they joined a small contingent already present, to improve the roads there and build ovens. In the meantime, he reorganized his own party before departing on October 10, finally arriving at a Miami Indian town three days later. On his journey, the captain received additional orders from Hamilton giving him wider latitude to finish his mission. So, MacLeod conducted his first significant round of diplomacy with the Miami Indians, who would be critical to the success of Hamilton's campaign.

While Clark had been brusque with the Native American nations in the Illinois Country, MacLeod stuck to the traditional formula: ceremonial pipe smoking followed by an exchange of long, indirect monologues. Gift-giving was usually a substantial element in diplomacy, but MacLeod was stingy, parting principally with rum and tobacco while holding the rest for

Hamilton. The captain's speech struck two themes. First, the Virginians were not as powerful as the Miami had been led to believe and need not be feared. Instead, they were weak and vulnerable, as evidenced by continuing raids on their settlements in Kentucky and their failure to advance to the Maumee. Second, MacLeod's presence was proof that the British were coming and remained committed to the Indian nations of the West.[16]

For their part, the Native Americans visiting MacLeod's camp were more reserved. While the Miami welcomed MacLeod and looked forward to receiving Hamilton, they were still concerned that Clark and the Virginians represented a threat to their homes as winter approached. Things might change when Hamilton actually arrived with an army. Fence-sitting was a strategically reasonable position given the rumors flying around the frontier.[17] Though affairs remained unresolved with the Indians, MacLeod continued his mission. Rain still plagued him as he prepared to haul supplies overland to a tributary of the Wabash. When it finally cleared, the Scotsman still faced the difficulty of finding horses healthy enough to haul carts or carry packs over the primitive trails that passed for roads.

While MacLeod and his men slogged through the rain and mud in September and October, Hamilton made his preparations, focusing on organizing his own men and raising Indian allies. Finally, on October 7, he set out from Detroit with roughly 165 soldiers and militiamen, seventy or so Indians, and one 6-pounder gun mounted in a bateau, plus as many supplies as his boats would carry.[18] It was not a large force, but still exceeded the number of men Clark had initially taken west from the Falls of the Ohio. His passage was only slightly better than MacLeod's. On October 9, Hamilton recorded sleeting rain and snow, yet he

> proceeded till 11 at night, very cloudy with rain, I began to be very apprehensive at [as] the wind rose and a heavy swell rolled in, we were on a lee shore and it was extremely dark—I determined to put in shore as soon as the sternmost boats could come in sight of a light which I carried in the headmost boat—my anxiety for their safety increased every instant, at length I rowed in for the Shore, and was happy to find it no worse than a swamp which took us to the knees.[19]

It was a truly rough night that could transform a knee-deep swamp into a welcome refuge for men already tired and soaked to the bone by pelting rain, sleet, and snow.

Whereas MacLeod had proceeded uncelebrated up the Maumee, Hamilton's arrival provoked welcoming ceremonies among some of the Indian nations who had heeded the lieutenant governor's call to take up arms in 1777. Ojibwe, Odawa, and Miami villages and warrior bands all welcomed him. By October 25, Hamilton finally caught up with MacLeod and his work teams at the portage. Hamilton endorsed MacLeod's work over dinner, but his mind was focused on the growing number of Native Americans in the area, assembling both to receive his gifts and learn of his plans.[20] He then held a meeting with leaders from the Odawa, Miami, Ojibwe, Wyandot, Miami, and some Shawnee. After showing around his war belts from tribes farther afield, Hamilton "produced a road belt, by which they were to understand that I should proceed to any part where the Rebels might be found, in order to dispossess them, and that the road should be constantly kept clear of all Incumberances."[21] With winter approaching, he was a man in a hurry.

Word from other nations across the frontier arrived over the following days, encouraging each other to unite and repel the Virginians. In truth, a great many of them offered little in the way of warriors. They were waiting to see whether the British or the Virginians would gain the upper hand. Hamilton would still have to depend on his English, loyalist, and French soldiers and the Great Lakes Indians who did much of the fighting and raiding against American settlements. He might grow that force with a substantial addition of Miami Indians and others settled along the Wabash, who had been the objects of much of Clark's diplomacy. (Indeed, Hamilton was unable to sway the Piankeshaw band led by Big Tobacco's son, with whom Lieutenant Helm had already built a loose alliance.)

CHAPTER TEN

Hamilton on the Wabash

October 27, 1778 to December 17, 1778

*I*t *was difficult for both* MacLeod and Hamilton's forces to haul their
supplies from Detroit to the storehouses at Miami Town. Nevertheless,
across rough water, through pelting rain, and against the Maumee's current,
they had done it. The British had brought foodstuffs, ammunition, trade
goods, and all the accoutrements of war to supply an army, secure Indian
participation in the offensive to retake Vincennes, and build a base for future operations to retake the Illinois Country. Logistically, it was quite a
feat for warfare on the American frontier, often requiring backbreaking
work unloading tens of thousands of pounds of wet goods, drying them,
repacking them, and then reloading them. Repeatedly. But that was the nature of moving even this small army hundreds of miles in a dense and un-
developed wilderness limited to travel on rivers or small footpaths and game
trails. It was about to get much, much worse.

Since arriving at the portage, Captain MacLeod had focused on improving the land route between the headwaters of the Maumee and a trib-

utary of the Wabash. That meant cutting timber, removing stumps, widening paths, building bridges, filling ruts and washouts, building storehouses, assembling carts, and any number of tasks associated with moving an army overland. Reaching Vincennes by water would take more work under worse conditions.

On October 29, Lieutenant Governor Hamilton left his camp and ventured down to the creek where his army would launch its boats into the water. The sight was disturbing. Hamilton wrote:

> This creek is one of the sources of the Ouabache and takes its rise in a level plain which is the heighth of land near the Miamis Town—the creek is called petite riviere. Where the pirogues were first launched it is only wide enough for one boat and is much embarassd with logs and Stumps—about 4 miles below is a Beaver dam, and to those animals the traders are indebted for the conveniency of bringing their peltry by water from the Indian posts on the waters of the Oubache.[1]

To complicate things further, tree branches overarched the small waterway. Over the years, root networks had spread into the water from below while trunks and branches fell in from above, making it impassable for the heavily loaded pirogues that Hamilton needed to move downstream. Last, but never least, the tributary was a winding creek. Some of the bends were so short that some of the pirogues, as much as thirty-two feet long, could not make the turn. MacLeod and his axmen went to work.

Besides removing trees in, on, and under the water, the British took an idea from the beaver to make things go faster. They cut breaks in the dams wide enough for a boat to pass but narrow enough to be easily closed by laying a boat crosswise or using sod and a handful of paddles. The result was a primitive lock system in which they could raise and lower the creek's water level to move the boats downstream. It was primitive, strength-sapping work in the cold water, but it was an improvement over the constant cargo unloading and loading work they had done in the driving rain along Lake Erie's coastline and up the Maumee River.

Still, moving down the creek for another ten miles remained a struggle. Having gotten past the worst twists, Hamilton bemoaned, "we were yet worse off . . . coming to a swamp called les Volets, from the water lilly which almost covers the surface of this fen—The bateaus frequently rested on the mud, and we labor'd hard to get thro', being up to the knees in mud and entangled among the roots and rotten stumps of trees."[2] Hamilton was fortunate in that he needed to spend the bulk of his army's advance negotiating with various Native American nations, enlisting allies, reassuring waverers, and reaffirming old relationships. Not so for MacLeod and his soldiers, who had to wrestle the pirogues through mud and muck, around narrow turns, and over fallen trees for days on end, amid temperatures that constantly fell. MacLeod's diary entry for November 7 described a typical day:

> This morning embarkd at Seven and arrived at Twelve oClock, made a little halt then Proceeded and enterd the Shallow Country where the water was Very Shallow and the River full of large Stons and Rocks. Every man was in the water draging till Seven in the evening whene we was obligd to Encamp, hardly two Boats together and the men so fatigued that they were Scarce able to mount guard.[3]

The next morning, they had to unload half the supplies to draw less water before they could start the same process again.

As the army progressed, creeks joined the Little River, which eventually made its way to the Wabash. The deeper water made it possible to use oars more frequently and make better time, but periodic rapids and the weather conspired to complicate travel just the same. Snow fell on November 11 and the river surface froze solid in places by November 22.[4] Progress required bashing through the ice and dragging boats through water up to the men's knees, with the ice often cutting them.[5] That, combined with the river's natural obstacles, battered the boats and Hamilton's army was frequently forced to lay up and make repairs. To lighten the load, Hamilton offloaded some supplies onto horses and had them parallel the river over difficult portions. Of course, that meant still more backbreaking work in awful conditions shifting cargos and reloading the boats downstream. Ice continually plagued the rest of the advance, forcing men to stand frequently in freezing water while they manhandled the rough-hewn vessels over rocks and through ice.

The contrast with Clark's advance could not be more stark. The Virginians had certainly enjoyed better weather. By traveling light, primarily over wider rivers, they could move more quickly, even at the risk of empty bellies during their overland march from the Ohio River to Kaskaskia. Hamilton was encumbered by the need to present supplies and gifts along the way to the Indian allies he thought he needed to gather. Here, the lack of reliable intelligence about Clark and his force imposed a considerable cost. Hamilton left Detroit with a force roughly the same size as Clark's Virginia militia. But, unsure of what faced him, the lieutenant governor was compelled to rely on Native Americans both to augment his numbers and secure their continued participation as belligerents on the British side. The larger his force and the more numerous his allies, the easier it would be for Hamilton to counter Clark's diplomatic efforts to neutralize Indian participation in the war. While the added troops might serve as insurance against surprises from Clark's side of the equation, they necessitated more supplies that slowed Hamilton's progress and exposed him to worsening weather. Thus, November found MacLeod's men wrestling heavy boats through ice-choked shallows while Clark's men enjoyed the relative comfort of frontier cabins and autumn harvests.

While MacLeod focused on logistics, diplomacy occupied Hamilton. Representatives from a range of Indian nations came and went, updating Hamilton about the latest intelligence on the Virginians, other tribes, and the best routes forward. As important, the lieutenant governor learned more about the consequences of earlier British indifference to the Illinois tribes:

> These Indians as well as the Illinois, and Misouri Tribes, have been kept almost altogether in the dark with respect to the power of the British Nation, few but contemptible Renegadoes from the English having been seen among them, & the French Traders from interest as well as a mortified pride, decrying as much as possible every thing that was not French.[6]

So, while Hamilton might rely on his Indian allies from the Great Lakes region, the Native American inhabitants of the country he was entering—and among whom Clark had concentrated much of his diplomacy—remained an open question. The British settled in at Ouiatenon for Hamilton to collect his strung out forces, repair boats, gather additional information, conduct more diplomacy, and prepare for the last leg of his trip to recapture Vincennes. Arriving chiefs conceded that they had been intimidated by Clark and smoked the peace pipe with the Virginians, whom they thought were present in considerable numbers. Clark's campaign of intimidation and deception had worked. But, with Hamilton's forces in the area local tribes quickly backtracked and agreed to join his campaign. Finally, on December 5, Hamilton began his descent on Vincennes in earnest. With the arrival and renewed alliance with various Native American nations, Hamilton's aggregate army had grown to roughly six hundred men.[7]

As Native American scouting parties joined and departed Hamilton's army, bad weather continued to plague it. On December 8 intensifying winds marked a front passing through. It dumped so much freezing rain and snow on Hamilton and his army that the men had to start fires inside

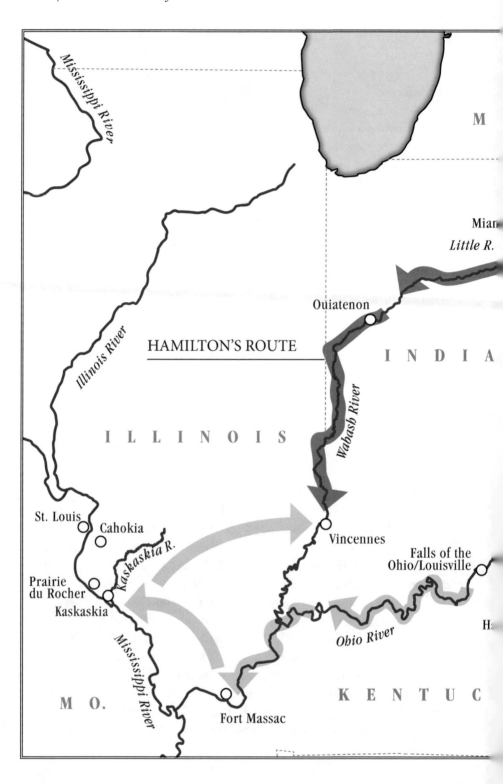

Detroit

H I G A N

LAKE ERIE

Maumee R.

The Glaize

Auglaize R.

P A.

Pittsburgh

O H I O

Monongahela R.

CLARK'S ROUTE

Ohio River

Limestone Creek

Kentucky River

W. V I R G I N I A

Boonesborough

rg

V I R G I N I A

their tents to thaw them enough for stowage.[8] Despite the weather, on most nights, contingents from the various Native American nations accompanying Hamilton held elaborate war ceremonies and debated their own approach to waging war. They preferred to camp a mile or so away from the British. Warriors also preferred raiding to the slow, steady movement of Hamilton's army. So, Hamilton employed them as scouts ranging on both sides of the river to hunt, collect intelligence, and intercept any scouts that Clark's men might have watching the river. Unfortunately, the hunting often involved taking shots at wildfowl nesting along the Wabash. The gunfire was as likely as Hamilton's boats to alert any Virginians watching the river. The day after thawing their tents, during one volley loosed at a flight of turkeys, an errant shot struck the Shawnee leader White Fish in the eye, putting it out. Though undoubtedly in pain, apparently White Fish's only regret was that he had lost the eye to friendly fire, rather than in a standup fight against the enemy. Hamilton used the incident to extract a promise from the Indians to exercise more firing discipline.[9]

On the approach to Vincennes, Hamilton's attention shifted from diplomacy and logistics to combat. Weapons' repairs, inspections, drill, and security took up more of his army's time and energy while he cajoled the Indians to scout farther ahead. Nevertheless, snow continued to taunt his men while ice clogged the river. Anxieties rose among the Native Americans accompanying Hamilton's force. He reported a growing number of foreboding dreams among them.

On December 15, Hamilton sent a reconnaissance party down the ice-choked Wabash with orders to pass Vincennes and take the town's measure. They returned quickly with four prisoners: Lieutenant Brouillett and three men who had been sent with similar instructions by Captain Helm, the commanding Virginian at the renamed Fort Henry, previously known as Fort Sackville. Brouillet had the misfortune of holding a commission in the town's militia from both the Virginians and the British. Hamilton, however, did not hang the man lest it "whet the natural propensity of the Indians for blood" and out of a desire to bring Brouillet back to the British side.[10] He might need the French as much as Clark did. Summarily hanging a local would only encourage them to resent the return of British forces. The bulk of the information he received as he approached Vincennes indicated that the Virginians had largely left the area for the winter, that only a few officers remained at the fort, and that defense depended mainly on the local French militia that had sworn allegiance to the Americans that summer.

The British lieutenant governor divided his force into four units. He sent one group of Indians west to cover the paths and roads from Kaskaskia to Vincennes and another east to interpose itself between Vincennes and the Falls of the Ohio. Their tasks were simple: intercept any information leaving Vincennes and provide warning of anything approaching. A third group led by his second in command, Major Jehu Hay, would advance on the town. Among others, Hay's force included a detachment of Captain William LaMothe's Detroit-based militia and the 6-pounder cannon. Some of the Indian forces he had gathered along the way would join them, although Hamilton remained concerned about their discipline upon entering the town and fort. So, Hamilton held back the bulk of the Native Americans still with his army. The British aim was to recapture the town intact and return it to British control, not destroy or alienate its residents. If Brouillet's information proved accurate, the lieutenant governor also expected Helm and his few men to take the opportunity and flee. Hay would occupy an empty fort. Hamilton would follow by water with the remainder of his troops and Native American allies.[11] It was late, so Hay did not embark his troops until December 16.

At Vincennes, Captain Helm knew Hamilton was coming and close. He had dispatched Brouillet to collect more intelligence and was aware that the lieutenant had been captured. So, Helm dashed off a note to Clark letting his commander know. He had worse news to share. The local militia, which had surrendered to Father Gibault, taken a loyalty oath in July, and then welcomed Helm's arrival in August, opted not to turn out. They would switch sides. Again. Helm observed, "I have but 21 men. . . . I feel not four men that I can really depend on but am determined to act brave. . . . I know it is out of my power to defend the town as not one of the militia will take arms."[12] Sent as Major Hay's men occupied the town on December 17, Hamilton's scouts intercepted the letter.

When Hamilton roused his command the same day, the wind was blowing snow again. With his scouting forces out and Hay in the town, however, Hamilton still needed to reach the fort. Not only was it key to the reconquest of the Illinois Country, but the weather must have reminded him that winter was upon him and the campaigning season was rapidly coming to an end. The fort and town promised a respite from the wet, near-frozen state his men and supplies had spent much of their time in since leaving Detroit.

About a mile north of the fort, Hamilton encountered Hay's boats pulled up to the shore, secured only by a small guard party. Seeing the

American flag still flying in the fort, he feared that the French militia had turned out for Helm, the Virginians had been reinforced, or both. Ordering his men ashore where Hay had landed, the lieutenant governor found a small rise from which he could get a better view of Fort Patrick Henry/Sackville. There, he spotted Hay and his men drawn up near an old Indian village, where they were collecting arms surrendered by Vincennes' citizens, including the militia. Hay had already forced the town's surrender, but Helm remained in the fort.

Hamilton approached the outer works, his men arrayed for battle behind him and the 6 pounder up front. Hay had already communicated with Helm, who would not strike his colors until he knew the terms of surrender. Having no power to resist, the lieutenant could only insist on formalities. He sent out a note asking who demanded the fort's surrender, requesting the response in writing. Hamilton instead sent a verbal message, identifying himself as the lieutenant governor. With that, Helm met him at the outer works. Hamilton offered only humane treatment for Helm and his men, pointing out that Helm was not in a position to ask for anything.[13] Accepting reality, Helm admitted Hamilton into the fort.

Terms were not a mere formality, although his attacker's rank and the official terms were a matter of honor for the lieutenant. The promise of British military protection and humane treatment could be matters of life and death for Helm and his men. In eighteenth-century warfare, garrisons putting up a futile resistance could expect to be plundered, a process often involving atrocities by their adversaries. On the frontier, with the added mixture of Native Americans, prisoners could expect to be tortured, massacred, or sold into slavery, as had happened during the French and Indian War and Pontiac's War. With long experience on the frontier, Helm was already familiar with Indian treatment of prisoners. Hamilton knew it as well and the fear worked to his benefit, just as fear had worked for Clark. Indiscriminate looting and violence were always a possibility when Native Americans were involved in a successful attack. (They were elements of the war in the East, as well, but professional training and discipline attempted to hold them in check.) That was one reason Hamilton sought to disperse his Native American allies with scouting missions while Hay captured the fort.

With that in mind, Hamilton's "first care was to place centrys at the Gate to prevent the Savages getting in."[14] His effort to prevent a quick plundering failed. Some of the younger Indian warriors with him ignored the lieutenant governor and their leaders and entered the fort. Their success started a general rush. Seeing their fellow warriors on the inside, those outside overpowered the British sentries and rushed the gate. They set off a stampede of horses inside, each Indian looking for his own new mount. Hamilton used the chaos to set a guard on Helm's quarters, but Indians broke through windows in the rear and took what they wanted. Helm warned that there was a barrel of rum in the house, which Hamilton's guards did manage to secure before its consumption escalated things from looting to violence.[15] Fort Sackville was back in British hands. Hamilton was pleased with his success, writing in his diary, "Not a single shot was fired in the course of the day, nor did the Savages commit any excess but plundering the horses in the Fort—Guards were mounted, and patroles orderd to pass thro' the Village every hour to prevent accidents."[16]

Hamilton assessed the state of the fort's defenses and was decidedly unimpressed. Fort Sackville was a picket fort constructed in the usual way: digging a deep ditch, standing stripped and split tree trunks vertically in the ditch, and then filling it in so the trunks stood upright. There was no firing platform running the length of the wall for small arms. The artillery consisted of two iron 3-pounders mounted on truck carriages and two unmounted swivel guns. It even lacked a well. If Helm was aware of Hamilton's critique, he might have pointed out that the British built the fort.

After holding a ceremony marking Britain's recapture of the town, Hamilton paroled Helm and set about improving the fort. The British dug a well, erected bastions, and built barracks and a gatehouse for the winter. He distrusted the local population and did not afford them the same self-governance that Clark had. Hamilton intended to govern with intimidation, informing the locals that he had only spared their lives because they had voluntarily disarmed. It was a reasonable posture. After all, loyalty was not their strong suit. Indeed, rumors continually poured in that the Americans were coming, prompting Hamilton to conclude, "As I have since had reason to believe the inhabitants of the Post were determined upon betraying me on the first opportunity, I must suppose these reports were raised either with the view of seeing what measures I should take in case of an attack, or by repeating false information to make me inattentive to all alarms."[17] He had to settle for requiring them to take another oath of allegiance, placing little confidence in it. He later noted, "It is scarce to be wondered at, that the inhabitants of this remote place, (a refuge for debtors and Vagabonds from Canada,) should be lost to every principle of probity and honor, when they were under the influence of so worthless a mortal as the Ecclesiastic Gibault."[18]

His attitude was a misreading of the psychological battlefield. Hamilton thought in terms of allegiance and loyalty. But those were the terms in which British interaction with the town was on its weakest foundation. The population was largely French. Its primary experience of British governance was indifference. Indeed, the lieutenant governor appointed for Vincennes, Captain Abbott, had only remained in his post a few months before departing, leaving the community to fend for itself and conduct its own affairs. By promising to leave that situation largely untouched, Clark had not won the town to his side, so much as enabled a small detachment of his men to occupy the fort and fly Virginia's flag from the pole. All the while, he took extraordinary measures to project strength and ruthlessness while asking little from the local community itself. Self-interest and in its own way, independence, guided the people of Vincennes. Rather than recognizing and exploiting those facts, as Clark had, Hamilton could only view changing allegiances through the lens of loyalty and disloyalty, leading to his lack of trust in the community. At the same time, his need to winter over at Vincennes in order to resume his campaign in the spring meant that Hamilton still depended on the town.

The situation was the same with the local Native American nations. With Hamilton ensconced in Fort Sackville, the local tribes drifted away from the Americans with whom they had at least reached some form of accommodation and returned to the British camp. The Piankeshaw leader Grand Coete, or Old Tobacco, and his son met with Hamilton, who reproached them for drifting toward the Americans. They blamed Hamilton for having holed up in Detroit when the Americans first came, leaving the Piankeshaw to face American strength by themselves. Grand Coete argued, "When the Rebels came into the country I was alarmed, what I have done was from a sense of my own weakness."[19] Clark's campaign of intimidation had worked, but only as long as his threat remained credible. From the Piankeshaw standpoint, Hamilton's army in its midst represented a bigger challenge and a new reason to align with the British. The episode confirmed for Hamilton, however, that he was not surrounded by allies, whether French or Native American. Even the Great Lakes Indians, upon whom Hamilton had relied during the war, warned him of it.[20] (They, of course, did not face the immediate threat of Clark and his Virginians.)

Unlike Clark, who had projected strength from the American Bottom, Hamilton was about to surround himself with evidence of weakness. Despite his attitude and arrogance toward the locals, white and Indian alike, Hamilton eventually rearmed them and dismissed many in the Detroit militia, who were anxious to return home. More troops, and the most reliable Indians, were not far behind. Captain MacLeod was among them. By the end of January, Hamilton was down to ninety-six men.[21] The lieutenant governor would rely on the defenses of Fort Vincennes and the local militia, which he disdained and had already proven unreliable, to winter over before resuming his campaign to recapture the Illinois Country in the spring of 1779. Back on the Mississippi, George Rogers Clark had no intention of waiting.

CHAPTER ELEVEN

An Alarm in Kaskaskia

December 1778 to January 29, 1779

*I*n June 1778, while Clark's little army was making its way down the Ohio toward the Mississippi, a congressional committee investigating unrest in the Ohio Country recommended a campaign against Detroit from Fort Pitt. In October, while Clark was settling in along the Mississippi, Brigadier General Lachlan McIntosh launched his offensive, leading roughly 1,200 men, mostly militia, up the Beaver River before turning westward. Clark knew this campaign was coming—it was no secret when large numbers of men assembled on the frontier—so he assumed that the army Hamilton was gathering at Detroit was bound eastward to repel McIntosh, rather than south and west to reclaim the Illinois. The conclusion led his men to "Injoy ourselves for the first time since our arrival."[1]

Hamilton, of course, had already set his sights on the Wabash and MacLeod was on his way south almost a month before McIntosh left Pittsburgh. While his army slogged overland from Pittsburgh, Hamilton rendezvoused with MacLeod at the portage. The British were busily raising and lowering water levels on a freezing tributary of the Wabash when McIntosh gave up entirely, stopping to build a fort and supply depot on the Muskingum River (today known as the Tuscarawas), before returning to Pittsburgh. He ostensibly planned to renew his overland offensive in the spring. Clark eventually learned of McIntosh's about-face from people coming up from the Falls of the Ohio with Clark stating that it "disappointed us very much."[2] Nevertheless, McIntosh's aborted campaign had distracted Clark from what Hamilton was really doing that autumn.

Clark circulated among the towns on the Mississippi in December, checking on his men, showing his face among the locals, meeting with Indian leaders, and collecting news from passing traders or Indians. But he grew anxious at the lack of news from Vincennes. Helm was supposed to communicate every two weeks, but Clark heard nothing. So, the Virginian sent spies and couriers. None returned. Hamilton's Native American allies and scouts were doing their jobs well. Thus, the Americans were in a state of suspense as they moved up and down the Mississippi.[3] The relative sense of ease created by successful rounds of diplomacy among the Native Americans and McIntosh's campaign dissipated.

Against that backdrop of uncertainty, after a days-long snowstorm trapped him in town, Clark finally set out from Kaskaskia bound for Cahokia. A short distance down the road, Clark and his party spotted several men in the distance but could not discern who they were or what they were doing. They were likely townspeople, but the possibility of spies or a hostile war party could not be dismissed. Curiously, Clark and his men came across chairs periodically abandoned alongside the road as they approached. Finally reaching the group, they learned where the chairs had come from and why. The group they had been approaching was from town. One man was struggling to get his carriage out of a ditch, while everyone else stood by, laughing. No doubt the man whose carriage was stuck had lightened his load by abandoning his cargo as he moved down the road. The ridiculousness of the scene raised spirits as Clark continued on to Prairie du Rocher, where he intended to spend the night.[4] The lieutenant colonel later learned that an Indian scouting party watched the entire affair from the safety of the woods. He believed they had opted not to attack him out of fear.[5] Clark had every reason to include the story in his memoir as a way of heightening the drama of his would-be bestseller. None of that takes away from the fundamentals of the story, the small amusements of everyday life pregnant with potentially imminent violence, or the trinity of Frenchman, Virginian, and Indian in the Illinois Country.

After a pleasant supper with Captain Barbers in Prairie du Rocher, someone proposed a dance. At the height of the revelries, an express arrived informing Clark and his men that a group of Black woodcutters on the Kaskaskia River had encountered a group of white men and Native Americans. The whites told the woodcutters, likely enslaved, that there were eight hundred of them nearby and they intended to attack Kaskaskia, then threatened that anyone disclosing the information would be put to death. The report, of course, was not strictly true. Hamilton did have scouts in the region, but nowhere near the reported number. The threat may have been concocted for any number of reasons: keeping the Americans on edge, forcing them to take shelter in their forts, reminding unreliable locals that the British and their allies had not given up on the area, or simply testing the woodcutters. Clark, however, was still operating in the dark and had no way of knowing their intent. He chose to treat the report as factual. His response is typical of the bravado he maintained to bolster the reputation for fierceness that had contributed to his success. Several men attempted to persuade Clark to cross the Mississippi and seek sanctuary on the Spanish shore. He laughed off the idea and announced his intention of returning and entering the fort at Kaskaskia.[6]

While his men dressed in borrowed clothing to disguise themselves as simple hunters, Clark maintained an outward sense of lightness and amusement while pondering his next actions outside in the moonlit, snowy landscape. After a few minutes, he dashed off a note to Captain Bowman at Cahokia ordering him, his Virginians, and all the locals he could raise to cautiously join him at Kaskaskia. He also left Bowman the option of retreating across the Mississippi to St. Genevieve, a French-dominated town in Spanish territory, if circumstances dictated.[7] Clark ordered the messenger to run his horse to death if needed to deliver the message as quickly as possible.

Clark and his men arrived outside Kaskaskia the next day, fully expecting to find it and the fort under siege or occupied. Taking a circuitous route around town to scout for enemies, they found none and entered. Clark was convinced the snow had put off the British and their Indian allies. Still believing that an attack was imminent, he concluded that Vincennes must have fallen, for the British would not have passed it by before striking for the Mississippi. Clark expected Kaskaskia's population to honor its summertime loyalty oath to the Americans and summoned the town's leaders to consider their next steps. Just as the residents of Vincennes had abandoned Lieutenant Helm, the citizens of Kaskaskia now abandoned Clark, who wrote, "after some deliberation they told me that they thought it was prudent to Remain Nutral."[8] Clark did not fault their logic. After all, he had occupied the American Bottom through surprise and intimidation, not by force of arms. His small contingent of Virginians were spread all across the region and vulnerable; and the rumored British force in the area reportedly outnumbered his own and the local militia combined.

Rather than meekly accepting Kaskaskia's neutrality, Clark turned to his usual tools: boldness and intimidation. "I pretended to be in a passion," he recalled. Then he dismissed the town's leaders and told them he would burn portions of the town to improve the fort's defenses. When some younger, local militiamen did turn out for him and recommended that he bring supplies from the town into the fort, Clark sent them home, proclaiming he had enough provisions to face the British. It was another act of daring, reinforced when he burned a barn full of grain near the fort's walls. Afterward, the Virginians began clearing a field of fire by dismantling buildings, bringing wood into the fort, and burning structures from which an attacker might find cover. "[A]ll was now confution the Town on Fire the women and Children screaming moving &c I sensibly felt for them."[9]

As he had before, Clark engaged in a bit of psychological warfare to advance his cause. Amid the chaos of burning buildings, some citizens approached Clark asking how much of the town he intended to burn. He replied that he would burn only those portions necessary to fulfill his duty to defend the fort and to deny the British any supplies. Then he announced he would suspend burnings until the wind shifted so that the fire would not spread out of control. Clark also lied, telling them that an army from Kentucky was approaching and would intercept any British and Indian forces marching toward Kaskaskia. By raising concerns about the shifting winds and presenting a threat to the rest of the town, he also transformed himself into a potential savior of the town's wealth, much as he had simultaneously created a threat and positioned himself as a relief from it when seizing Kaskaskia in the summer. Of their own volition, the citizens asked for and received permission to move their household goods and provisions into the fort.[10] In two hours, enough carts rolled voluntarily through the front gates to supply the Virginians for six months. Even allowing for exaggeration, Clark had obtained the stores he might need without seizing them or appearing to need them. The tactic was simple: "To make ourselves appear as daring as possible."[11]

After clearing the fort's fields of fire and preparing for a siege, things in Kaskaskia began to calm down. Scouting missions determined that the rumored British force was a mixed group of British and Indian scouts, likely one-tenth of its reported size, and already departing the area. The next day,

Captain Bowman rode in from Cahokia, bringing his Virginians and some of the local militia.[12] Together, the two officers concluded that Vincennes had fallen.

Although the moment had passed, Clark still found himself in a tenuous position. The locals on whom he relied for security and had gone to some great lengths to secure for the American cause, revealed themselves to be wholly unreliable, even with his men in town. It was probably no surprise. On the other hand, those few militiamen who had ridden from Cahokia with Captain Bowman might prove the core of a more dependable security force. He rewarded them with better clothing and arms, which they promptly paraded before the residents of Kaskaskia, leading to some ill feelings.[13] It was just one of the psychological games Clark played during his campaign, rewarding loyalty and encouraging competition for his favor among local factions.

With that, Clark settled in to await news from his own scouts prowling the country between the Mississippi and the Wabash. While he waited, the Virginian settled on a contingency plan. In the event that Hamilton approached with a large number of troops and the Virginians could not hold their positions, they would abandon the American Bottom and retreat to Kentucky, whose population exploded throughout the war. Then, knowing that the Native Americans who most likely dominated the British force did not engage in long campaigns, Clark would raise a new force in Kentucky and seek to get between Hamilton and Detroit. In effect, he would upend their roles, a strategic reversal that spoke well of the Virginian.

On January 29, Francis Vigo arrived in Kaskaskia, and he had a tale to tell.

CHAPTER TWELVE

A Few Men
Well Conducted

January 30, 1779 to February 23, 1779

*F*rancis Vigo was a St. Louis merchant and trader, not to mention business partner of Spain's lieutenant governor for Upper Louisiana, Fernando de Leyba. The lieutenant governor and Clark had arrived in the
region at about the same time and hit it off.[1] They shared an interest in
weakening British control of the Mississippi and moving supplies from
Spanish territory to the Americans, whose supply lines via the Ohio were
vulnerable. With that in mind, Clark hired Vigo to transport supplies to
Lieutenant Helm at Vincennes. Hamilton's Indian scouts picked Vigo up
en route.[2]

Vigo was one of those frontier personalities who contributed to the Mississippi basin's distinctive multinational flavor and made it a colorful cross-
roads of nationalities, ethnicities, cultures, and languages. He appears to
have been born in Mondovi, Italy, in 1747 and joined the Spanish Army
sometime in his youth. Dispatched to Cuba and then to New Orleans when
Spain took over the west bank of the Mississippi, Vigo eventually found

himself in St. Louis. He had reason to know de Leyba. They had both spent time in Cuba and lived in New Orleans.[3] At St. Louis, the pair found in each other an opportunity for advancement. De Leyba, who witnessed French fur traders making money all around him, was unable to partake due to the official demands of his office. Vigo, on the other hand, was in a position to make money in the fur trade but needed the imprimatur of Spanish officialdom. A business partnership made eminent sense. Vigo became the de facto agent for distributing Spanish gifts to Native American tribes in the area, giving him the opportunity to build a network and the potential for future profit in trade.[4] So, it was natural for de Leyba, Vigo, and Clark to see their interests align in cross-river trade once the Virginian arrived in Illinois at the end of a perilously long and vulnerable supply line. Clark could strengthen the relationship with de Leyba by contracting with Vigo to supply the Americans in the Illinois Country (Some writers suggest that the burgeoning cooperative relationship between de Leyba and Clark had as much to do with Clark's interest in the lieutenant governor's daughter Teresa as with any alignment of interests, but there is scant evidence for it.)[5] Because neither the Americans nor the Spanish along the Mississippi knew Hamilton had already recaptured Vincennes, Vigo must have been surprised to find himself facing the British lieutenant governor.

Interrogated by Hamilton, Vigo accurately related the weakness of the American position along the Mississippi. Hamilton could rest easy for the winter. Since Spain and Britain were not at war, the lieutenant governor released Vigo to return home to the Spanish side of the Mississippi, provided he promise not to reveal his observations at Fort Sackville to the Americans on the way. Vigo lived up to the letter of his promise. But, after a stop in St. Louis, he recrossed to the American side and met with Colonel Clark on January 29. His was the first eyewitness confirmation that Vincennes had fallen to the British in December. The Italian reported that Hamilton was in the fort with thirty regulars and fifty French volunteers, plus various Indian agents, boatmen, and the artificers needed to keep an army functional. Some four hundred Indians had been with Hamilton, but Vigo knew the lieutenant governor was sending men home. Most important, he revealed Hamilton's plan to winter at Vincennes and then resume his offensive toward the Mississippi in the spring.[6] The Americans were in no immediate danger. They had time to consider their options and act. So, they called a council.

As was becoming his habit, Clark quickly read the strategic situation. His position on the Mississippi was untenable in the long run while Hamilton controlled Vincennes. Worse, if Hamilton was reinforced in the spring and brought together another large force of Native Americans from the North and, possibly, the South, the Virginian believed the Americans incapable of gathering an armed body capable of resisting it. Kentucky would fall and Hamilton would be free to run rampant across the frontier.[7] It was exactly how Hamilton saw affairs when gathering his army to retake Vincennes. So, as usual, Clark leaned into the problem, preferring to seize the initiative. (Within the space of a few pages in his memoir, Clark had given up his earlier thought of getting between Hamilton and Detroit. There could be a range of explanations for the change of attitude: failing memory, brainstorming options versus making informed decisions, ex post facto analysis of his options, or even ill-disciplined drafting of his book.) In any event, his first instinct—to seize the initiative—is apparent, as is his ability for more thoughtful analyses over time.

Since Hamilton would receive reinforcements in the spring, he was at his most vulnerable in the near term, despite being well ensconced in a fort that his men were improving every day. As Clark recalled, "we saw but one alternative which was to attact the Enemy in their Quarters If we ware fortunate it would save the whole if otherways it would be nothing more than what would Certainly be the consequence if we should not make the attempt."[8] The more he thought about it, the more Clark liked the idea. He wrote Patrick Henry, "I am resolved to take advantage of his [Hamilton's] present Situation and Risque the whole on a Single Battle."[9] Boldness and surprise had served the Virginians well thus far. They might serve again. He wrote later, "The Enemy could not suppose that we should be so mad as to attempt to march 80 Leagues through a Drownded Cuntrey in the Debth of Wintor that they would be of[f] their Guard and probably would not think it worth while to keep out spies that probably that if we could make our way good we might surprise them."[10]

Having made the decision, Clark moved quickly. As he had when seizing Kaskaskia, Clark would march overland, taking the least expected route in order to surprise his enemies. Fortunately, the earlier scare at Kaskaskia had already forced the Americans to prepare for battle and better arm the local volunteers from Cahokia. They returned with Captain Richard McCarty on February 4.[11] It was only at that point that Clark asked for volunteers from Kaskaskia and received the town's support stating, "The whole of the Inhabitants Exerting themselves in order to wipe of past Coolness."[12] In short, Virginia's fair-weather friends in Kaskaskia were friends again. The men who joined his command from Kaskaskia would serve under Captain

Francis Charleville, bringing the total army up to 170. Clark planned to travel quickly, which meant traveling light, relying on packhorses, and dispensing with boats, carts, or wagons. He eliminated tents entirely, despite the weather.[13] At least the men he took to the Wabash would be well-armed and supplied, if not living in the lap of campaign luxury. It meant, however, that they would be marching with only the supplies they could carry into hostile territory as the local Indians returned to the British. Failure at Vincennes would strand them without supplies in the middle of winter. Fortunately, Clark had a contingency plan.

He purchased and armed an American row batteau, which he christened *Willing* after James Willing. Lieutenant John Rogers would take command and drop down the Kaskaskia River to the Mississippi, then follow the Mississippi to the Ohio. From there, he would ascend the Ohio and Wabash to take a post ten leagues below Vincennes, where he was to await further orders. The *Willing's* presence was to be kept secret. Clark instructed, "Suffer no vessel to pass you except friends . . . keep spies on the bank of the rivers as you go up them, for fear of surprises."[14] Rogers' mission was to prevent Hamilton from fleeing down the Wabash. The *Willing* was also heavily armed with one 9-pounder, two 4-pounders, and four large swivels. Perhaps as important, she carried ammunition and supplies. Clark could call upon her should he need them.[15] Rogers and his crew departed the afternoon of February 4.

Clark assembled his forces by February 5. In deference to the local religious practices, they received a "lecture and absolution" from the local priest before crossing the Kaskaskia River bound for the Wabash. Temperatures were reasonable, but conditions were drizzly. Mud and water plagued the men at every step. After a solid nine hours of marching, they established a camp in the shape of a square, with baggage collected in the middle. Individual companies camped together in the formation and were responsible for providing their own guards. The army sat in camp for three days, waiting for the rain to stop and the land to dry a little. It was a pointless exercise. So, on February 8, the army broke camp early and set out through the water. Spirits remained high, but conditions were already fatiguing the men.[16] At Vincennes, Lieutenant Governor Hamilton noted the Wabash was rising rapidly.[17]

It was a slow trudge across Illinois. The rain persisted, but at least the temperature was warm. By the time the army reached the Petit Fork on February 10, the river was so swollen that fording was not an option. Finally, someone came up with the idea of cutting trees down and dropping them in the river. The improvised footbridges worked, and Clark's men crossed to the other side. Without tents and amid storms, the men settled in for another long, wet night. To the east, at Vincennes, Hamilton noted, "The river continues to rise considerably." A pirogue from the Illinois Country also arrived that day. It had been fifty days in transit.[18]

Clark crossed the Saline River on February 11 and finally reached a broad plain the next day. He noted that "a great part of the plains was under water for several Inches," while Bowman recorded that "the Road very bad from the immense quantity of rain that had fallen. The men much fatigued."[19]

Through the water and the inevitable chafing it caused, Clark turned his attention to keeping up morale. While he could probably count on the Virginians, the militia drawn from Cahokia and Kaskaskia that made up nearly half his force might be less reliable. After all, the Kaskaskians had already abandoned him at just the threat of a British attack. How might they act after a long, demoralizing march at the end of which lay a confrontation with the lieutenant governor, his regulars, and hostile Native Americans? To address this challenge, he allowed hunting during the march and charged each company in turn with holding a feast at the end of each day. The company hosting that day's event received extra horses to make it easier to haul any bounty taken. By spicing up the feasts with "Indian war dances" Clark's party reached the Little Wabash without any hints of disgruntlement.[20]

If the hunting contests and nightly feasts cooperated with the warm, but wet, weather to maintain morale in Clark's little army, its spirit was about to be sorely tested. When he arrived at the Little Wabash, about three miles west of the Wabash River proper, Clark discovered a vast watery plain stretching five miles into the distance. The river channels were not discernible, and Clark estimated the water was three feet deep, certainly no less than two and as many as four in some places. Somewhere under that expanse of water, a river waited. Despite having walked across a soggy Illinois, often in ankle-deep water, the men had not encountered anything quite so intimidating. The Virginian found a slight rise in the land that at least enabled his men to gather out of the water and contemplated his situation.[21]

Bravado, commitment, a little bit of daring, and the casual dismissal of obstacles, whether they involved corralling mutinous men on Corn Island, intimidating residents of the American Bottom into surrender, or bringing Native American nations to the peace table, had brought Clark this far. They would again. Clark "Viewed this sheet of Water for some time with

Distrust but accusing myself of Doubting I amediately Set to work without holding any consultation about it or suffering any body else to do so." He ordered the men to build a pirogue "and acted as though crossing the water would be only a piece of diversion."[22] Because only a few men at a time could work on the dugout, Clark found ways of occupying everyone else's attention. Still, his anxiety grew as the work progressed. It was obvious that once they crossed the water, they would largely be trapped in the event of failure. Retreat would not be an option. While Clark's men worked, Hamilton noted that the Wabash continued to rise at Vincennes.[23]

The men finished the boat the next day, February 14, and sent it off about four o'clock in the fading light of a winter afternoon in search of unsubmerged land, or at least some rise where they could camp.[24] The scouts identified half an acre as far as five miles away that would serve and blazed a trail by marking trees on their way back to Clark's camp. The army waded to the patch of ground above water the next day, relying on the pirogue to carry ill men and some baggage. In one particularly deep spot, the men built a scaffold on which to pile baggage while the pirogue and horses plunged forward. The column naturally strung out as men felt their way through the water, relying on marks blazed on trees, the ferrying pirogue, swimming horses, men nearby, and a drummer boy who floated much of the way aboard his drum. By evening, they had finally crossed the watery expanse to ground high enough for a camp. Morale remained high, according to Clark, as men congratulated themselves on quite the exploit. Clark encouraged the celebratory mood and pride in the accomplishment: "they really began to think themselves superiour to other men and that neither the Rivers or seasons could stop their progress."[25] In that mindset, Clark's men joked that the Wabash channel would prove little more than a creek and their attention turned to the spoils that might be won at Vincennes. Naturally, they had passed the day in a steady rain. Clark ordered men not to fire their rifles to maintain secrecy.

February 16 and 17 proceeded much the same for Clark and his men. But the vast plain of water was nearly devoid of game and the men dug deeper into their stored goods, some of which were undoubtedly ruined by the constant water—falling from the sky or underfoot—they had slogged through since leaving Kaskaskia. Those provisions began to grow noticeably short.[26] Clark's attention, however, shifted from maintaining morale and keeping the men moving forward to dealing with Vincennes and Lieutenant Governor Hamilton. He surrendered all hope of approaching the Wabash over dry ground, accepting his fate that the "whole of the Low

Cuntrey on the waubach was drownded" and concerned that his men were vulnerable to an attack from Vincennes.[27] His only aid might come from Lieutenant Rogers and the *Willing*, expected to be on the Wabash farther down by now. Then, of course, there was the Wabash itself to find and cross. With that in mind, he dispatched five men to cross the Embarrass River and strike out for a plantation on the west side of the Wabash, where they might find and/or steal some boats and canoes to get across the river. The mission failed and the army kept groping forward, looking for a way to cross the Embarrass and reach the Wabash. By default, they ended up following the Embarrass River toward its mouth on the Wabash. They traveled well past eight o'clock at night, in darkness, mud, and water, until finding a small spot of ground from which the water at least receded a bit. It became camp for the rest of the night.[28]

At dawn on February 18, Clark and his army heard the bark of Fort Sackville's morning gun marking the time. Clark found it amusing, for there was still no sign that the British or their allies had detected his little army.[29] It undoubtedly confirmed for many what they already knew intellectually: their adversary was perilously close. They continued marching down the Embarrass until two o'clock that afternoon, finally reaching the Wabash about three leagues below Vincennes. Their challenge now was to get across the largest river they would encounter. It might well prove an impossible task. The army quickly assembled a raft to sneak four men across in search of boats. They never found dry land.[30]

Lieutenant Governor Hamilton, who had tracked the water's rise for a week, noted that the White River, not far away and farther down the Wabash, had flooded so much that its normal 250-yard width was nearly a league. As for the Wabash, it was so far over its banks that cattle were lost due to the flooding. Locals had set off as far as twenty miles in pirogues in search of livestock that might have escaped the flood. The river had backed up streams to a local sawmill, which could not operate. Meanwhile, opposite Fort Sackville, the depth had increased from ten to thirty feet. Hamilton noted, "The South side of the river appears like a lake for two leagues below the fort."[31] But, the warm weather also brought spring. Peach trees were blooming about Vincennes and apple trees had already sprouted their first buds. As Clark reached the opposite shore a few leagues away, Hamilton noted that his men made noticeable progress on the northwest blockhouse at the fort.

On February 19, Captain McCarty's men built another canoe. While they were working, the men who had attempted to cross on a raft the day before finally returned, having spent the night in the water. Then it was McCarty's turn to cross with three men in his newly fashioned canoe in an attempt to steal some boats from the other side. He was not gone long before returning after spying four large fires about a league distant from where Clark's men were camped. Three attempts to find boats locally had failed. Clark promptly dispatched two men in the canoe downstream to find Lieutenant Rogers and the *Willing* with orders to bring it up the river as quickly as possible. Morale, which had remained high, began to suffer in the face of the flooded Wabash, exacerbated by short supplies. Joseph Bowman noted in his diary, "Many of the men cast down, particularly the volunteers. No provisions of any sort, now two days."[32] The entire campaign would unravel if Clark could not get his army across the swollen river.

The morning of February 20 did not bode well for Clark. Bowman noted, "Camp very quiet but hungry; some almost in despair; many of the Creole volunteers talking of returning."[33] Clark laughed at them but did not argue or order them to stop discussing such an option. Instead, he told them they should go out and hunt. It seemed to do the trick for the moment. Maintaining confidence in his core of Virginians, Clark still thought he had a few days before the French militiamen would turn for home. Meanwhile, "I conducted myself in such a manner that caused the whole to believe that I had no doubt of suckcess." With the possibility of deer meat by the evening meal and the chance that the *Willing* might arrive any minute with fresh supplies, Clark expected he had bought some time.[34] In the meantime, the men started making more canoes.

Things looked brighter still when a sentry brought a boat with five Frenchman aboard to shore. They were favorably inclined toward the Americans and reported that Vincennes' residents were as well. Hamilton's haughty treatment in December rankled. Better still, they shared the latest intelligence about the fort and garrison and alerted Clark to some abandoned canoes upstream. A search party managed to retrieve one. Best of all, they confirmed that the British were completely blind to Clark's presence. Meanwhile, the French militia Clark had dispatched earlier in search of deer found some with luck and returned to provide a solid meal.[35] In Vincennes, Hamilton noted that the river had fallen a foot.[36]

On February 21, Hamilton turned his attention to another round of Indian diplomacy, holding a council of assembled Odawa, Wyandot, Delaware, Miami, Ouiatenon/Wea, and Piankeshaw nation leaders at the fort. The Piankeshaw leader, Young Tobacco, was on the agenda. Lieutenant Helm had made progress swaying Young Tobacco and his father away from the British and Hamilton chastised the Indian after reconquering Fort Sackville in December. Now it was the turn of the other Ohio tribes and representatives from the Lake Indians to pressure the Piankeshaw leader face-to-face. Cornered, Young Tobacco again declared his commitment to the British and their Native American allies, blaming his earlier missteps on his youth. The council broke up when messengers announced that a Huron and two Miami warriors had arrived from a trip to the Falls of the Ohio with a scalp and their victim's rifle.[37] As the hour was getting late, Hamilton announced they would reconvene the next day.

As the sun rose on the same day, Clark and his army began crossing the Wabash on two canoes.[38] Conditions were still daunting, and the packhorses remained on the western bank. The only dry spot was a small hill called "Mamel" and the army attempted to dry out as men collected on it, piled their baggage out of the water, and Clark's newly made canoes did their work ferrying people and supplies back and forth. Hunger was a common problem. Supplies had been damaged during the march and game remained scarce in the flooded Illinois territory.[39] About a league away and across a depression, Mamel rose higher into something Clark called "Upper Mamel." The interval was flooded. While looking for some way across, Captain Williams and two of his men spotted two strangers in a canoe, who simultaneously spotted the Americans. Williams could neither lure them close nor catch them. Clark's ability to hide his army was falling. There was no other option. He had to act quickly and led his men into the water, striking out for the Upper Mamel, often up to their armpits in still more muddy river water.[40] Clark originally hoped to reach the town on the twenty-first, but the crossing, deep water, and more rain scotched his plans.[41] With no sign of the *Willing*, the men made camp and went hungry again.

Clark's men faced another day of empty bellies, water, and despair on the twenty-second. Some of the Frenchmen they had taken on February 20 told Clark about a sugar camp on the banks of the Wabash that would bring them closer to Vincennes. It rose above the water and became Clark's next destination. He sent a canoe to reconnoiter a route, only for it to return and report the intervening waters were too high. Determined to decide for himself, he paddled in that direction as well and found the water as deep as a man's neck. Turning around, but with few alternatives, he planned to use the canoes to ferry his men across, a time-consuming effort that would take all day and night as the canoes had to navigate tangles of bushes. The prospect of going another day without food was disheartening. "I would have given now a good deal for a Days provision or for one of our Horses." Clark returned slowly to buy himself time to work through the problem.[42]

As Clark paddled up in his canoe, his army quickly gathered around, eager for his report. To Clark's regret, someone overheard him discussing the problem with one of his officers. "[T]he whole was alarmed without knowing what I said the[y] ran from one to another bewailing their Situation."[43] By now, Clark's reliance on audacity was second nature. He whispered to those nearest to follow his lead, then blackened his face with gunpowder, gave a war whoop, and plunged into the water without another word. According to Clark, "the party gas[p]ed and fell in one after another without saying a word like a flock of sheep." He ordered those nearest to begin singing and the tune spread from man to man so that "the whole went on cheerfully."[44] Captain Bowman simply noted, "Col. Clark encourages his men, which gave them great spirits."[45] After a short while, when the men were waist deep, one reported that he thought he felt the outlines of a path beneath his feet. Clark and his officers concluded it was the real thing and likely the shallowest water around. They followed it to the sugar camp and found about a half-acre above the water, their latest in a long line of damp, muddy camp sites. Once there, Clark's French locals proposed going into Vincennes in both canoes, retrieving some provisions and additional boats, and then returning. He passed on the offer, not trusting its sincerity.

Back in Vincennes, Hamilton renewed his council with the Native American leaders then in town. He had procrastinated, but finally informed them that he had reason to believe Great Britain and France might soon go to war. It could be a test for British-Indian relations, as French influence remained strong on the frontier. He asserted, with reasonable confidence, that it would not much affect affairs in the Ohio or Illinois Country. He also expected them to treat the local French residents as "fellow Subjects," even though they had briefly joined with the Americans. The last thing he needed was an open rupture between the two communities, French and Indian, that preceded the English presence in the area. He depended on both to maintain any semblance of British authority. From Hamilton's perspective, his sudden announcement visibly struck the chiefs assembled in council, who renewed their pledges to the British side. But he suspected their reaction was merely an act as rumors had circulated for some time. In truth, word of the Franco-American alliance had already spread across the Illinois Country from Clark's Cahokia council and, more importantly, warriors returning from Montreal earlier in the year.[46] He was not telling those assembled in council anything they did not already know or suspect, merely confirming it. Visible reactions by the Native American leaders in council had more to do with maintaining the illusion of an old relationship that was quickly changing in fact.

On that day, Hamilton's men also completed the northwest bastion of Fort Sackville. Proper gunports could not be installed for a lack of iron, but they did mount a 3-pounder in the tower. Hamilton might have retired feeling more secure that night. However, in the afternoon, Francois Maisonville, who had been off chasing deserters, returned to Vincennes and reported that he had seen fourteen different campfires on the east side of the Wabash, just four leagues below Fort Sackville. These were most likely Clark's men at the sugar camp. Rather than risking capture himself, he did not venture closer, but concluded they must be Virginians. Hamilton agreed. He ordered Captain LaMothe to take his lieutenant and fourteen men to reconnoiter the report. Then he had ammunition sent to the blockhouses and set up an internal scaffolding for his small army at the north and south angles of the fort. The local militia was called to arms and all prisoners on parole, including Captain Helm, were ordered into the fort.[47] Nothing happened.

Rain plagued Clark's entire march to the Wabash, but at least it had been unseasonably warm. Now, on the night of February 22, temperatures fell precipitously. By the time the sun rose on the twenty-third, ice half an inch to three-quarters of an inch thick had formed along the shore of their little half acre and collected in the still waters of a plain before them. Called the Horse-Shoe plain, it stretched across some three to four miles, ending in a stretch of woods, beyond which lay Vincennes, Fort Sackville, and Lieutenant Governor Hamilton. It was the last major obstacle nature would throw at Clark and his men. The water was chest high. Clark gave a speech, reminding them how close they were, and plunged right in, leading his men toward the woods. They cheered and followed. But Clark was suspicious of a few. So, he halted and ordered Captain Bowman to take twenty-five of his men and station himself at the rear, where he was to kill any man summarily who refused to cross. Recalled Clark, "This was the most Trying of all the difficulties we had experienced."[48] Bowman's mind was elsewhere: "Never were men so animated with the thought of avenging the wrongs done to their back settlements, as this small army was."[49]

About halfway across, the water deepened, and it became difficult to maintain one's footing. There was nothing to hold on to: no bushes, no trees, no stumps. Clark became concerned that his weakest men would drown. So, he ordered the canoes ahead to deposit their baggage on a rise in the woods, after which they resumed ferry service, picking up the weakest men as Clark's army continued moving forward. He also pushed the strongest men to the fore, instructing them to turn about from time to time and announce that the water was getting shallower to those behind. Clark believed it boosted morale. As they finally made the woods, the water was still deep but there were trees and bushes to cling to or float on, shifting from place to place. The wooded rise, which Bowman dubbed Warren's Island, became their next stop, which they reached at about one o'clock. Some men were so exhausted they barely had strength to haul themselves out of the water before collapsing on "dry" land. Others set about making fires to warm themselves and dry anything possible.[50] Luck chose that moment to intervene. After a brief chase, some of Clark's men in a canoe captured some Indian women and children making their way to town in their own boat. The captured canoe contained "near Half Quarter of Buffaloe, some corn Tallow, Kettles &c."[51] A weak broth was the result, providing some of the first nourishment Clark's men had received in days.

Later in the afternoon, Clark's army turned to its overworked canoes again and shuttled across a narrow lake into another copse of timber on high ground known as Warrior's Island. The men had a full view of the town and fort through the trees. Clark recalled, "every man now feasted his Eye and forgot that he had suffered any thing that all had passd . . . it was now we had to Display our Abilities."[52] The object of their campaign and the point of a month's worth of suffering lay just in the offing.

CHAPTER THIRTEEN

Opening Moves in the Battle for Fort Sackville

February 24, 1779

Another damp field stood between George Rogers Clark and the town of Vincennes a mile or two away.[1] Still, it was drier than the lands his men had crossed thus far. Being uneven with slight rises and folds, pools of water had gathered in the depressions. Townspeople were out hunting ducks from horseback. Clark sent out some of his French militia as decoys to lure at least one hunter nearer, where he was successfully, and quietly, taken prisoner. Clark's latest local captive confirmed what the hunters taken earlier had told him, with the added information that the northwest bastion was complete and there were some six hundred men in town, including Hamilton's men, the local militia, and Indians.[2] Clark and his men were outnumbered by more than three to one. Even if the *Willing* arrived momentarily, the numbers advantage lay with Hamilton. So, he carefully prevented the hunter from seeing the strength of his army.

In what was perhaps a bit of ex post facto bragging, Clark claimed:

We ware now in the situation that I had Laboured to get ourselves in the Idea of being made prisoner was foreign almost to Every man as the[y] expected nothing but Torture from the savages if they fell into their Hands our Fate was not to be determined probably in a few Hours we knew that Nothing but the Most daring conduct could Insure suckcess.[3]

Things might not be as bad as they seemed. Clark thought he still had the element of surprise on his side and their prisoner apparently confirmed it. The Virginians could not conduct a long siege, however. It left too many things to chance. If he had enough supplies, the lieutenant governor could simply remain in the fort and await reinforcements. So, Clark turned to his favorite tactic: "I resolved to appear as daring as possible, that the Enemy might conceive by our behaviour that we were very numerous."[4] Clark also had reason to suspect the local French militia might prove unreliable to Hamilton. Some in town had found life under American government quite freeing as Clark essentially allowed them to govern themselves according to their own rules. If the militia stood neutral, as the militia at Kaskaskia had done to him just the month prior, that would seriously cut into Hamilton's numerical advantage. Ideally, some might even join his little band.

The wild cards he faced were the Indians in town. Clark had not anticipated them or Hamilton's conference. His understanding was that the Piankashaw leader Young Tobacco had defied the British and declared his allegiance to the "big knife," as the Virginians were known on the frontier.[5] Of course, Hamilton recorded it the other way around. But Clark's belief in the Piankeshaw leader, or his father, gave him additional reason to think audacity might just be enough to defeat Hamilton. So, he wrote out a notice for the citizens of Vincennes. It was an attempt to split them from the British, perhaps encourage a few defectors to his own army, and discourage Hamilton's soldiers.

The notice announced his presence and intentions to retake the fort. It further directed citizens to remain in their homes and urged those who still wanted to enjoy their liberty to join his army. Importantly, it also directed those who sided with Britain to join the garrison inside the fort and threatened severe punishment for any who were found on the streets under arms. Professed fearlessness and the threat of violence always hung in the air when the Americans first interacted with an enemy-controlled town and Clark urged those loyal to Britain to defend the fort and fight like men.[6]

He released the duck hunter with instructions to circulate the notice throughout town.

Next, Clark turned to deception, which had also served him well on the American Bottom and in his interactions with various Native American nations. He hoped the letter's arrogance would lead everyone in Vincennes to suppose there was a reason for his confidence, that his army was larger. Moreover, he hoped they would conclude his men were from Kentucky. The population there had continued growing, despite the war, and it could support a much larger force than the Americans along the Mississippi. Besides, everyone knew an army could not march from the Mississippi to the Wabash over such flooded territory in winter.

To that end, he had several of his men compose letters to friends under the names of individuals that the residents of Vincennes had every reason to believe were from Kentucky. The letters intimated that the American army was nearly one thousand-men strong. A messenger was dispatched into Vincennes with that correspondence and the Americans waited while all the news provoked a stir in town. Residents approached the edge to see what they could across the fields. While there was a commotion in town, Clark spied no activity in the fort, noting particularly that no long drum rolls or alarm guns were heard. The British, however, noticed the commotion in town and inquired. Suitable excuses were concocted, namely that LaMothe's men had drawn the town's attention.[7]

Those events took up most of the afternoon. With dusk approaching, Clark moved his men into the field and put his army on display for the town, but not immediately visible to the fort. He broke the army into two groups. Three companies, Captain Williams', Captain Worthington's, and the Kaskaskia volunteers constituted his first "division." The second comprised Captain Bowman and the men from Cahokia.[8] But, Clark still needed to disguise his numbers. So, he only revealed portions at a time, ordering a march and then a countermarch to appear more numerous. He used the terrain and intervening rises in the ground to further disguise his numbers, displaying various flags above the crest of the rise, without revealing that they did not represent any men.[9] Officers joined in by mounting horses that had been captured from more duck hunters and riding about over longer distances. Clark wrote, "in this manner we moved and directed our march in such a manner as to suffer it to be dark before [we] had advanced more than half way to the town." When darkness fell, Clark immediately changed direction yet again in order to appear behind the town and enter it from yet another direction. As the men moved into the densest part of town, he detached Lieutenant Bailey with fourteen men to march on the fort and bring it under fire.[10]

Inside Fort Sackville, Lieutenant Governor Hamilton waited while his men prepared, still unclear about the commotion in town. Maisonville's report and the disruption in town were enough to lead Hamilton to order a heightened state of alertness. He called on some militia, but still did not believe an army was moving against him. The Vincennes militia was slow to make its appearance. As darkness fell and the British completed their evening roll call, the garrison heard sporadic small arms fire in town. Hamilton dismissed it as the drunken firing of townspeople amusing themselves, despite hearing some of the "balls sing" as he went on to the parade ground. A British surgeon dining in town immediately ran for the fort when his host declared that Clark had arrived with five hundred men. He just made it, a bullet piercing his leggings but leaving him unharmed. After Lieutenant Bailey's men brought the fort under fire, Hamilton received a report that Sergeant Chapman of the King's Regiment had been mortally wounded. The news was in error—a button had deflected the bullet and saved the sergeant's life—but it dispelled any notion that the shooting beyond the walls was for fun. Hamilton, having already ordered the men to arms, now had them occupy the blockhouses and firing platforms, but with orders to conserve ammunition and only fire at what they were sure they could hit in the rapidly falling darkness.[11]

The battle for Fort Sackville had begun.

CHAPTER FOURTEEN

Great Things Have Been Accomplished

February 24, 1779 to March 5, 1779

Clark's little army kept firing at the fort all night while working its way
through the town to find the best positions from which to conduct its
siege. About 120 yards from the front gate turned out to be a good place
for an entrenchment, but the army started advancing breastworks closer to
reduce the range. They were simple hodgepodge affairs that could be
thrown up quickly by making use of material that was handy, but they were
built to leave places for cannon to fire upon the wall. Clark wanted to maintain the fiction that his was only an advance party of a larger army coming
up with artillery; he also wanted to be prepared when the *Willing* showed
with the few guns it carried. After reviewing their work, Clark and Captain
Bowman decided to start a separate engineering project along the river side
of the fort, hoping to undermine the walls the next night, perhaps creating

an opportunity to rush in from the river side after the wall collapsed or at least exposing the interior to artillery fire from the *Willing* should it make its appearance.[1] Overall, the town provided ample cover to move within range of the fort. Several men occupied a church and its yard, particularly the fence line, in addition to homes and barns. In hindsight, Hamilton regretted not burning them earlier and clearing his field of fire, but that would have complicated relationships with the town and its militia. Fires inside the fort backlit men securing the walls and moving about, so he ordered them put out. After one sergeant, one artilleryman, and two other men were wounded, the lieutenant governor moved them into the officer's quarters, where they might keep warm at the hearth. At the same time, the British used spare lumber and chinking to fill gaps through which light might pass.[2]

LaMothe's scouting party, sent out earlier to investigate Clark's fires at the sugar camp, returned to the fort when it heard gunfire. High water had forced them to take a circuitous route to the camp, so their return was equally meandering, and the group became lost. Clark learned of the mission and dispatched a party to intercept their return. LaMothe's men still made it to town and hid in a nearby barn, seeing some Americans pass close by. Around 4:00 a.m., when the fire slackened they rushed the external pickets, causing a panic among the garrison. Hamilton left his quarters when alerted that Americans were scaling the walls. He was relieved to find they were LaMothe's men climbing the external obstructions, arms in hand.[3] After the war, Clark argued that he decided to allow LaMothe's men to regain the fort because he preferred them inside the walls consuming supplies rather than outside them organizing pro-British Native American tribes.[4] Clark may have been taking liberties in his memoir. It was true that LaMothe could cause the Virginians considerable trouble outside the walls and had to be neutralized, which was why he had sent a party to capture LaMothe and his men. But it was imperative that Clark capture Fort Sackville quickly. He did not plan on a lengthy siege and the supposed benefit of LaMothe's men consuming supplies inside the walls was not outweighed by the increase in the number of its defenders.

Deception remained an important element in Clark's tactical repertoire. While keeping up a scattered, but continuous, fire on the fort, he created small reserve parties that would shift their positions around it. From each new position, they would periodically concentrate and increase their firepower and then jeer and laugh uproariously "as if the[y] had only fired on the Fort a few minute[s] for Amusement as if those continually fir[ing] at the Fort was only Regularly Relieved." In theory, the approach would keep the garrison "Eternally alarmed."[5] It may have boosted the self-confidence of his own men and also perpetuated apprehension among the locals and Indians around Fort Sackville. In truth, Clark lacked the manpower to maintain a tight perimeter around the fort and town. Gaps were extensive and inevitable. Clark's practice of moving men helped maintain the illusion of a larger army.

As the fighting continued, several of the most hostile Indians departed the Wabash, but they were never far from Clark's mind. The return of LaMothe's men to the fort may have ensured that the Frenchman was not out raising Native American tribes to fall on Clark's rear, but the Virginian well knew "we ware Daylel liable to [be] overpowered by the numerous bands of Indeans on the River in case they had again Hertily Joined the Enemy the certainty of which we ware yet unacquainted with."[6] It was another stroke of luck for Clark when the Native Americans abandoned Hamilton, preferring their strategy of continued ambiguity over one of decisive confrontation.

During the night, American relations with the town's residents began to deliver some benefits. Clark's efforts to catch LaMothe might have failed, but the warning indicates he had supporters willing to pick sides. Indeed, Captain Maisonville, who had reported Clark's sugar camp fires to Hamilton, ventured to a cousin's home in Vincennes to gather intelligence. The cousin warned Clark, who promptly seized Maisonville.[7] The two men who initially captured him hauled the Frenchman to the breastworks, tied him, and began firing from there, essentially using him as a human shield under the assumption that the British would not return fire. An officer eventually ordered Maisonville moved to a safe place.[8] (Somewhere along the line, the Frenchman admitted he had led Indian war parties on raids against Americans. One or more of Clark's men removed a portion of the man's scalp in retaliation.)[9]

Clark's situation improved when residents began sharing gunpowder and rifle balls from caches buried earlier to keep hidden from Hamilton. Some of the Vincennes militiamen even joined him. A few locals went so far as to feed his men a decent meal.[10] During the night, Old Tobacco even made an appearance, offering one hundred of his warriors to join in the siege by morning. Clark declined, telling the chief he had enough men with him and pointed out that there were other Indians about town who were hostile to the Americans. He was afraid of confusion about the two among the Americans. Instead, he invited the Piankeshaw leader to remain with him and offer counsel, which Old Tobacco did.[11] All things considered, the initial hours of battle were going well for the Americans. "Fine sport for the sons of Liberty," noted Captain Bowman.[12] Fire slackened in the early morning hours of February 24, as both sides prepared for the events of the day.

When the light rose enough to see on February 24, small arms and Hamilton's artillery in the blockhouses opened up on several of the buildings from which the British had received fire. Hamilton reported clearing homes next to the fort, but admitted two more men were wounded by Americans returning fire. Clark saw it differently. His soldiers had crept to the buildings nearest the wall, as few as twenty or thirty yards away. From his perspective, the cannon largely fired over the heads of his closest men. The defensive works the Americans built overnight, essentially a breastwork constructed by piling up material gathered around town, such as garden fences, largely kept them safe. Although one or two men were wounded, most of the damage was done to buildings farther away in town. Still, the Americans concentrated their small arms fire on the gunports, verbally taunting the garrison and daring the British to open the ports.[13]

During the fighting, Clark learned that two prisoners bearing letters had been brought into the fort on February 23. He suspected they were messengers bringing expresses to the American army, as he had expected someone about this time and had received no news in weeks. (They were, in fact, two Virginians traveling down the Ohio River whose papers did not contain "any thing essential" and had already been returned to them.)[14] The news prompted Clark to act. He had considered several variables throughout the night. Native American intentions were one. They could change without notice and he was quite vulnerable to their numbers. While the local white population had proved friendly or neutral, he was well aware of their fickleness. His limited number of troops was another. There were no replacements coming; the best reinforcement he could hope for was the *Willing*, about which he knew next to nothing since its departure down the Mississippi. He had a reasonable estimate of Fort Sackville's garrison and defenses, provided through observation, prisoners he had taken, and any updates that locals provided at the siege's opening, but he knew nothing about the state of affairs elsewhere. So, time was not on the American side. Hamilton could expect reinforcements that spring; Clark could not. Thus, news of new British prisoners prompted him to act.

Late in the morning of the twenty-fourth, he sent a local French militia captain under flag of truce to demand Lieutenant Governor Hamilton surrender the fort, its garrison, and any supplies therein. Different versions of

Clark's note and the time it was dispatched exist, but his summary was straightforward enough: "I sent a flag Demanding the Garison [surrender] and desiring Govr Hamilton not to destroy them with some threats in case he did if his Garison should fall into my Hands."[15] Firing then stopped and Clark's men received a full breakfast, refilling empty stomachs and restoring sorely tested constitutions.

Hamilton prepared his reply: "Lieutenant Governor Hamilton acquaints Colonel Clarke, that neither he or his garrison are to be prevailed on by threats to act in a manner unbecoming the character of British Subjects." Then he held an officer's call, read it to them, and announced he was determined to hold out to the last. They supported his position. So, he mustered the men on the parade and read both Clark's note and his reply. They cried "God save King George" and offered up three huzzas. The French militiamen, however, were less enthusiastic. There was considerable muttering among the men with their sergeants. Fighting would involve their friends and relations from the Mississippi on the other side, which they were none too eager to do. Just like that, half of Hamilton's modest garrison of seventy-nine men was unreliable and six of his men were already wounded.[16] The lieutenant governor's options were limited:

> Finding one half of my little Garrison thus indisposed, and that with so small a number as were well affected it would be absurd to think of holding out, that to retain the French was to depend on traitors, and to turn them out must give additional confidence to our Enemies[,] I determined from that moment to accept honorable terms if I could procure them.[17]

Clark's terms clearly did not meet those standards and Hamilton sent the reply he had already composed and read to the men. The firing resumed almost immediately and continued hotly for several hours. Refreshed by their breakfast and eager to put an end to the entire affair, some of Clark's men even proposed storming the fort.[18] The Americans took every opening they could to bring the fort under fire from multiple directions, creating a quasi-crossfire.

After a few hours of this, sometime near noon Hamilton raised a flag and dispatched Captain Helm with a letter proposing a three-day truce with no offensive or defensive operations while he and Clark conferred. He wanted a face-to-face meeting in which they each brought one assistant and maintained secrecy in their conversations. If Clark was unwilling to enter the fort, Hamilton offered to speak with him by the gate.[19] The American, of course, rejected a three-day truce, concerned that reinforcements might be on their way. He did, however, agree to meet with the lieutenant governor near Saint Xavier, the town's church. Captain Bowman would accompany Clark while Major Hay joined Hamilton. Captain Helm would also attend, although his status became controversial.

Around two o'clock, as Clark composed his response to Hamilton, an Indian war party and two sergeants of the Vincennes militia totaling fifteen to twenty men approached the outskirts of town from a hill to its rear. They had raided toward Kentucky to collect scalps and prisoners and appeared to have been successful. Seeing the British flag still flying over the fort in the distance and hearing no gunfire, they assumed all was well and shouted a traditional scalp cry announcing their success. Clark exploited their mistake by sending Captain John Williams and his men to meet and salute the returning warriors. The Americans returned the woops, as a welcoming party might be expected to do. As the Indians and their sergeants approached, they discharged their weapons in a customary salute. Williams drew near until an Indian leader grew suspicious. At that moment, the Americans attacked. Williams seized the leader as his men instantly changed roles from welcome party to dedicated enemy, firing into the approaching Indians. The Indians promptly fled, with at least one man killed, two wounded, and six made prisoner. (Clark, Bowman, and Hamilton all claimed different numbers in each category. These are Hamilton's claims and should be treated as a minimum.)[20] Two white prisoners with the Indians were promptly released.

In 1778, Clark had captured the American Bottom and Vincennes, recruited some of the local population to his cause, made diplomatic progress separating some Native American nations from their British allies, and developed a cooperative relationship with the Spanish across the Mississippi and in New Orleans. Although a careful cultivation of a reputation for ruthlessness was instrumental in his accomplishments, Clark's men had not actually committed significant violence in their campaign. The start of the attack on Fort Sackville the night before and Williams' effective ambush of the Indian war party changed all that. Now, Clark was about to demonstrate that the American reputation for ruthlessness was deserved. He explained to George Mason of Virginia, "I had now a fair opportunity of making an impression on the Indians that I could have wished for; that of convincing them that Governour Hamilton could not give them that protection that he had made them to believe he could."[21] Clark's next actions were not motivated by vengeance or blind racial hatred but had a calculated political purpose.[22]

Williams brought the captured warriors into town and Clark had them taken down the main road opposite Fort Sackville's front gate and in front of a house nearby. Captain McCarty, who Hamilton described as one of "Clarkes Banditti," recognized one of them as the son of an Indian who had saved his life and he was separated from the others. Of the remaining five, one was a white man, but Clark remained determined to execute him, even at the risk of causing dissension among his men. With that, soldiers from Clark's command, possibly including the colonel and at least one of his officers, started to tomahawk the remaining warriors to death in a summary execution. As the first Indian fell and the others realized what was happening, they began singing death songs. The white warrior cried out and Lieutenant LaCroix, an older Frenchman in Captain McCarty's volunteer company from Cahokia, recognized his son's voice. The relationship immediately created a dilemma for Clark. He was determined to make an example of the raiding party and quickly made himself scarce. Lieutenant LaCroix followed him, pleading his son's case. LaCroix had soldiered with him through so much adversity and the Cahokia militia contingent had been the most supportive of the American cause. He still needed their service and loyalty.[23] So, Clark gave in. The remaining four raiders, all Indians, were killed.

The last raider to fall was a young Odawa chief named Macutte Mong. The first blow did not immediately kill him, and the weapon lodged in his skull. The Odawa leader removed the tomahawk and handed it back to his executioner, who then struck him two more times. With their prisoners down, dead, or dying, the Americans dragged the bodies to the Wabash and threw them in. Hamilton reported that Macutte Mong was not quite finished and was pulled along to the bank with a rope around his neck. (Hamilton did not witness this episode, which occurred in front of a house where he was later quartered but was told of it by the building's owner.) Clark and Bowman were more succinct, stating simply that the Indians were tomahawked by the soldiers and then thrown into the river. According to Hamilton, "the Blood of the victims was still visible for days afterwards, a testimony of the courage and Humanity of Colonel Clarke."[24] Hamilton's sarcasm aside, Clark's opinion of the lieutenant governor was not any higher, unsurprising since he had become the focus of American hatred for Indian raids across the frontier after the June 1777 circular.

With the raiding party destroyed, Clark and Hamilton were ready to proceed with their face-to-face meeting. The executions appear to have changed the location, for rather than meeting at the church they met on a

parade ground in front of the fort. The lieutenant governor may have feared
for his safety after the recent display. Indeed, he moved some men into a
blockhouse with a view of the site with their pieces loaded and instructions
to keep a steady eye on the proceedings. For his part, Clark sat on the edge
of a batteau that still held some rainwater. Hamilton described him, "he
had just come from his Indian tryumph all bloody and sweating . . . and
washed his hands and face still reeking from the human sacrifice in which
he had acted as chief priest."[25]

Hamilton, who had already concluded he could not hold the fort, produced presigned articles of capitulation. Clark took note of one provision
that allowed the entire garrison to travel to Pensacola on parole. In the end,
he rejected every provision, insisting he could not retreat from his prior demand for surrender "at discretion," meaning unconditionally.

Clark continued by telling Hamilton bluntly that resistance was pointless and explained how he saw the situation. First, Clark informed Hamilton that his artillery would be up in a few hours. It was a bluff as he still
had no idea of the *Willing*'s whereabouts, but one for which he had gone
to great lengths to lay the psychological foundations. To that end, it was
important to stampede the lieutenant governor into a quick surrender. Second, he told the lieutenant governor he knew exactly what the fort's weaknesses were and on whom Hamilton could rely down to the last man. These
last points were reasonably accurate and confirmed by the local militia who
had rejoined the Americans. Hamilton knew them to be true. Since there
was no prospect of immediate relief for the fort, as Clark saw it, he could
only conclude that simple obstinacy explained Hamilton's refusal to surrender. Should the Americans be forced to assault the fort, "not a single
man should be spared."[26] He described such an action to Hamilton, by as-
serting "my Troops was already Impatient and Called aloud for permission
to tear down and storm the fort if such a step was taken many of Course
would be cut down and the Result of an Inraged body of Woodmen breaking in must be obvious to him it would be out of the power of an American
officer to save a single man."[27] The threat built upon the reputation for vi-
olent ruthlessness Clark had cultivated since seizing Kaskaskia, confirmed
by the recent executions.

Hamilton conceded he was outnumbered but insisted that his men were
reliable. Clark corrected him, highlighting that the lieutenant governor
could only truly depend on the regulars, and then played up his own numbers, arguing it was "folly" to think of defending the fort against such odds.
He repeated his earlier demand that Hamilton surrender "at discretion" and

then trust to Clark's generosity, promising better treatment than the British could expect under negotiated terms. It was the same approach he had used in the American Bottom and at Vincennes in 1778, where he had indeed largely kept his promises. The key difference, of course, was that in those instances he knew he would eventually need the locals, whereas the men before him now were British soldiers and the lieutenant governor himself. Still, there is reason now to believe that the promise was sincere in that Clark's force was smaller than it appeared, and he did not relish the prospect of managing so many hostile prisoners. Hamilton, of course, refused, saying he would not take a step so "disgracefull and unprecedented while I have ammunition and provision."[28] Clark promised Hamilton would be held responsible for the lives lost as a result, to which Hamilton responded his men would die with their arms in their hands.

Helm spoke up at that point, suggesting to both men that coming to reasonable terms would be preferable to spilling more blood. Clark turned on his officer, reminding him that he was a British prisoner and was in no position to address the subject. Hamilton immediately announced Helm could consider himself liberated from his prisoner's status. Curiously, Clark refused that privilege for his subordinate, insisting that he would not accept Helm's return at the moment, and he must return to the fort with the garrison. Clearly, Helm's attempt at mediation was unwelcome. Clark leaned into the all-or-nothing style of negotiation he had used on the Mississippi and did not want Helm to muddy the waters. Then Clark broke off the meeting, announcing a break to consider what had passed.

When they resumed, there was more of the same: Hamilton insisting he would only surrender on honorable terms and Clark demanding no terms but "at discretion." At various points, both men threatened to walk away, even starting back. During one such episode, Clark wrote that Hamilton stopped him. Bewildered by Clark's refusal to accept an honorable surrender, he asked why. Clark's response is worth quoting at length:

> I knew the greatest part of the principal Indian partizans of DeTroit was with him that I wanted an excuse to put them to Death or other ways to treat them as I thought proper that the Cries of the Widows and Fatherless on the Frontiers that they had occationed now Required their Blood from my Hands and that I did not chuse to be so timorous as to disobey the absolute Commands of their authority which I looked upon to be next to divine that I would rather Loose Fifty Men that not to Impower myself to Execute this piece of business with propriety that if he choose to Risque the massacre of his Garison for their sakes it was at

his own pleasure that I perhaps might take it in my head to send for some of those Widows to see it Executed.[29]

Major Hay asked whom Clark considered Indian partisans. Blunt as ever, Clark replied to the major with his own name. In truth, he undoubtedly meant a broader swath of British officers, essentially those who directed and participated in the Indian war. As the Indian agent under Hamilton, Hay's name would be high on the list. But he surely was not alone. According to Clark, Hay blanched while Hamilton blushed. If we can place confidence in Clark's description, it may have been the first time Hamilton confronted the possibility of being held accountable for the kind of frontier war he had advocated. He surely already understood the consequences intellectually. Prisoners were routinely brought to Detroit and scalps taken during the war presented to him at each Indian council. But it had been in the abstract. Now he faced a different kind of consequence in the visible anger of George Rogers Clark and Joseph Bowman.

The braggadocio notwithstanding, both Clark and Hamilton had an interest in finding some accommodation. Their discussion thus far had more to do with attempts to outbluff one another by constantly raising the stakes than with intimidating one another into simply giving up the battle. Whether Clark's speech changed Hamilton's thinking such that he decided there was greater risk in resisting American fury than in trusting Clark's mercy, which it must be remembered Clark had demonstrated in every town captured thus far, or the lieutenant governor simply decided he had held out as long as he could, it was time to end the discussions. Hamilton returned to the fort with a promise from Clark that fighting would not resume until a signal gun had been fired, giving both sides an opportunity to prepare beforehand. With both commanders returned to their posts, there was one more exchange of terms and an agreement was finally reached. They were simple enough:

1. That Lieut. Col. Hamilton engages to deliver up to Col. Clark, Fort Sackville, as it is at present, with all the stores, &c., &c., &c.
2. The garrison are to deliver themselves as prisoners of war, and march out with their arms and accoutrements, &c., &c.
3. The garrison to be delivered up at 10 o'clock tomorrow.
4. Three days' time to be allowed the garrison to settle their accounts with the inhabitants and traders of this place.
5. The officers of the garrison to be allowed the necessary baggage, &c., &c.

Signed at Post St. Vincents, 24th Feb., 1779

Agree to for the following reasons: The remoteness from succors; the state and quantity of provisions, &c.; unanimity of officers and men in its expediency; the honourable terms allowed; and, lastly, the confidence in a generous enemy.

Henry Hamilton, Lieut. Gov. and Superintendent.[30]

Clark's reasons for delaying the handover until February 25 were simple. By the time their discussions ended, and terms were agreed to, it was late in the day and sunset was approaching. He did not want to risk the uncertainty of a handover in the dark and needed time to prepare for occupying the fort, processing prisoners, and dealing with the militiamen who had joined Hamilton's garrison.[31]

The British did not raise their colors the next morning to be spared the humiliation of hauling them down. Around ten o'clock Captains Bowman and McCarty's companies paraded on one side of the front gate. Governor Hamilton and his garrison, arrayed in full uniform with shouldered arms and bayonets gleaming, marched out. Colonel Clark then led the companies of Captains Williams and Worthington into the fort, where they relieved the sentries, secured the arms, and hoisted the American colors. Hamilton turned about, marched back to the front gate, closed it, and rejoined his soldiers. Fort Sackville, now Fort Patrick Henry, was once again in American hands. Clark issued orders for the fort's 6-pounder to fire thirteen rounds to honor the thirteen states. Unfortunately, one of the baskets holding cartridges exploded through some accident. The explosion burned Captains Bowman and Worthington plus four privates, two of whom were British. According to Hamilton, one of the British privates had most of his skin "blown from his face and arms" and was nearly blinded, although he recovered well enough to march away with the rest of the garrison when it left Vincennes as prisoners. The explosion further displaced the log work an inch and a half and threw one Frenchman entirely over the wall. After falling ten feet, he was spry enough to land on his feet and run to his officers boasting of his alertness.[32]

After the ceremonies were complete, Clark inspected the works and concluded Hamilton had indeed been as vulnerable as the Americans hoped. In the afternoon, he gathered some of his officers and Lieutenant Governor Hamilton in a small room inside the fort. Clark asked which officers had been employed with the Indians, that is, which officers had accompanied Indians on raids. Hamilton declined to provide names and announced that said officers were present and would answer for themselves. Once they had done so, Clark directed the blacksmith to prepare irons for the neck, hands, and feet of every single one. Hamilton asked to meet separately with Clark and then protested the order as incompatible with the terms of the surrender. He pointed out the incompatibility of allowing him to walk about armed while slapping his officers in irons. Then he went so far as to challenge Clark's honor if he followed through. When Clark remained unmoved, Hamilton reminded him that the lieutenant governor himself had issued the orders and Clark might as well throw Hamilton in irons. Clark, who had listened with growing impatience, abruptly broke off the conversation and ordered Chabert, Reaume, LaMothe, and Maisonville placed in irons.

Relations between the Americans and the British captured at Vincennes worsened the next day as well. One Frenchman, who had served as a militia volunteer in British service and accompanied the Indians on raids, was brought into the fort with a rope around his neck. The Americans were in the process of hanging him when French militia who had marched with them from the Mississippi and fought at Fort Sackville intervened and he was hauled down half choked.[33] Still, Clark could not afford to alienate everyone in Vincennes and needed to lessen the challenges of managing his prisoners. He permitted some of the town's citizens, who had proved unreliable to him and Hamilton both, to rejoin the local militia. A few days later, he allowed some of LaMothe's men to return to Detroit on their parole, even providing boats and supplies for the trip.

Most importantly on February 26, Clark acted on information that a supply convoy was imminently expected from upriver. He sent Captain Helm and Majors Bosseron and Legraw/Legare with fifty militiamen in three armed boats upriver to intercept the convoy. The next day, the *Willing* finally arrived at Vincennes. Things were well in hand, but the additional supplies, artillery, and reinforcements only strengthened Clark's position. (It also brought word of Bowman's promotion to major.) Perhaps because of that, he discharged the captured British officers on parole on March 1. It rained the next three days, but on the morning of March 5, Captain Helm and his men returned. Their mission had succeeded in taking seven provision-laden boats and forty prisoners, including a judge and commissary from Detroit. Most importantly, perhaps, the convoy carried letters from correspondents in Detroit dated early February. They revealed a town underdefended with low morale and eager to have its lieutenant governor return. Indeed, Clark's attention had already turned to Detroit. For him, the Illinois campaign was over. It was time to take the war to the seat of British power in the West.[34]

Epilogue

Clark's war did not end with the Illinois campaign. Although the next logical strategic step was to take control of Detroit, the seat of British power on the western frontier, Clark lacked the resources. He turned to the Continental Army, attempting to coordinate with forces at Fort Pitt under the command of Colonel Daniel Brodhead while seeking support from Virginia. Brodhead agreed with Clark's analysis and sought to convince General Washington to support a two-pronged drive against Detroit from Pittsburgh and Kentucky in 1779. While Washington appreciated the situation, he deemed a campaign against Fort Niagara and the Iroquois nations allied with Britain more important. He directed Brodhead to give up immediate designs on Detroit and support Major General John Sullivan's march into Iroquois territory.[1]

Clark found Virginia just as frustrating. Rather than supporting his designs against Detroit, the state diverted troops to a campaign against the Cherokee to the south. Meanwhile, Colonel John Bowman, the Kentucky County lieutenant, led his men north against the Shawnee capital of Chillicothe. While Bowman did not defeat the Shawnee outright and his offensive resembled a raid rather than the kind of campaign that Clark envisioned, it did result in the death of Chief Black Fish.[2] At the same time, Virginia's credit in Illinois and with the Spanish across the Mississippi River began to run out. Simply, bills went unpaid too long. So, Clark returned to Louisville in August, his first time back in Kentucky in more than a year. There, he learned that Captain Joseph Bowman, who had proven so critical to the Illinois campaign's success, succumbed to the burns he received when the cannon blew up in Fort Sackville, one suspects from an infection.[3]

While the Americans remained paralyzed, Indian raids across and along the Ohio River continued. Despite a harrowing winter of 1779/1780, whites continued pouring into Kentucky, perhaps reassured by Clark's victory on the Ohio, the survival of Harrodsburg and Boonesborough through the war's earliest years, and the ever-present appeal of land and opportunity. The county's population might have been as high as twenty thousand by the end of the summer in 1780[4]

With Spain's entry into the war in 1779, Britain launched a two-prong assault on the West in 1780. A combined force of British regulars, Indians, and militia assembled at Prairie du Chien and advanced down the Mississippi under the command of Emanuel Hesse, bound for St. Louis to attack a small garrison there led by Clark's old acquaintance, Lieutenant Governor Fernando de Leyba. Across the river at Cahokia, one of Clark's former captains, John Montgomery, commanded American forces. While Montgomery and de Leyba sought to coordinate their efforts, they were significantly outnumbered by the combined forces advancing upon them. In May 1780, Hesse arrived outside St. Louis and led the bulk of his forces against de Leyba and the French militia at the battle of Fort San Carlos. He dispatched a smaller, but still significant Native American force across the Mississippi to attack Cahokia. The British approach was no secret and Clark arrived at Cahokia a day ahead of the attacking Indians. His reputation for fierceness earned during the Illinois campaign paid dividends and the Indians retreated, unwilling to press their attacks.[5]

Britain's second avenue of attack that year aimed squarely at Kentucky. Captain Henry Bird crossed the Ohio with some eight hundred Native Americans and small pieces of artillery. Although Bird intended to attack Louisville, rumors that Clark was in town led the Indians who constituted the bulk of his invading force to prefer easier pickings in two Kentucky settlements: Martin's Station and Ruddell's Fort, both north of the Kentucky River. They fell in June, while Clark was inspecting Fort Jefferson at the confluence of the Ohio and Mississippi Rivers. Despite hurrying back, he was unable to raise a force and catch the war parties as they retreated across the Ohio with hundreds of prisoners, dozens of whom were killed along the way.[6]

The raids prompted the Kentucky militia to mobilize and concentrate in larger numbers than usual for a campaign under Clark's command against the Shawnee. He crossed the Ohio River at the head of one thousand men on August 1, bound for Chillicothe. Finding that town abandoned, he burned local buildings and crops then pursued the Shawnee to Piqua, where they had concentrated. There, the Kentucky militia and Indians fought a significant battle. Clark, who had hauled artillery the entire distance, used it to drive the Indians out of a log fort while trying to flank their line of retreat. Rough ground foiled the flanking maneuver and the Indians eventually retreated from their town. Clark and his men looted what they could and burned the rest. Then, with their victory in hand, the Kentuckians withdrew back across the Ohio. Despite winning the battle and driving the Shawnee away from Kentucky, Clark had not decisively defeated them, and they continued raiding along and across the Ohio River.[7]

Clark continued to fixate on Detroit, knowing it remained the center of British power in the West. He returned east that fall to seek political and material support for such a campaign from Virginia. While Governor Jefferson embraced the idea, recruiting efforts that winter failed miserably. Meanwhile, Virginia garrisons in the Illinois Country began to collapse for lack of provisions. The few soldiers at Kaskaskia abandoned the post, leaving it to the local militia, which was disgruntled. The soldiers in Vincennes went on half rations. In June 1781, the Virginians abandoned Fort Jefferson at the confluence of the Ohio and Mississippi. By August, Clark more or less gave up and departed Fort Pitt, taking some four hundred men back down the Ohio toward Kentucky. A force of Pennsylvania militia led by Colonel Archibald Lochry followed but was largely wiped out when it put ashore near the mouth of the Miami River.[8] If British neglect helped facilitate Clark's successes in Illinois during 1778 and 1779, American neglect threatened to undo them.

Unfortunately for Clark, the growth in Kentucky's population diversified its centers of political power. Whereas a young and charismatic George Rogers Clark could influence the small fortified towns of Harrodsburg, Boonesborough, and St. Asaph in 1777, more voices paralyzed decision making and Kentucky's new leaders could not agree on a decisive course of action. In October, as American troops besieged Yorktown, Clark wrote Governor Nelson, "I have lost the object that was one of the principal inducements to my fatigues & transactions for several years past—my chain appears to have run out. I find myself enclosed with few troops, in a trifling fort, and shortly expect to bear the insults of those who have for several years past been in continual dread of me."[9]

Short of men, material, and money, Clark did the best he could in 1782, but had no practical way of taking the initiative. Kentucky's border was simply too long and accessible for him to defend. In August, a substantial force of Native Americans and British Rangers crossed the Ohio and laid siege to Bryan's Station. They could not overwhelm the fortified town's defenders but burned outbuildings and crops in the area before withdrawing. Kentucky's new leaders threw together a scratch force of militia to pursue them and fell into a trap just across the Licking River at the Battle of Blue Licks, considered by some the last major battle of the American Revolution. Although he was nowhere near the battle, defeated officers and their political allies maneuvered to place blame for the defeat on Clark's head. Nevertheless, Clark's commitment to Kentucky persisted and he assembled another army of some one thousand men in November and crossed the Ohio River yet again, invading Indian territory. This time, the Native Americans retreated before him and did not make a stand as they had at Piqua. Clark and the Kentuckians were reduced to burning towns, despoiling crops, and carrying off any goods they could find.[10] Such was the nature of frontier warfare, regardless of which side did the attacking.

The Treaty of Paris may have ended the American Revolution, but the war on the frontier continued. Native American nations north of the Ohio River raided along and across it, albeit without the wartime support of Great Britain. During the war, Virginia lost or failed to pay many of the bills Clark had incurred on the frontier and he was held personally liable for the debts. Consequently, he was destitute.

Things only worsened for Clark after he was caught up in a 1786 expedition to confront a burgeoning confederation of Native Americans along the upper Wabash River. With the states, Congress, and territorial authorities working at cross-purposes, a planned offensive proved feckless, and Clark became a scapegoat for its failures. He demanded a formal inquiry, but the Virginia Council condemned him without a hearing. Simply, Clark had acquired political enemies, and they never missed an opportunity to undermine his reputation, capitalizing on what was likely a growing problem with alcohol. In an attempt to escape his financial straits, Clark worked on a draft of his memoirs, but he never completed them. Instead, he took a personal interest in a new town chartered on the north shore of the Ohio

River, across from Louisville. Named Clarksville in his honor, he served as a trustee and as president of the Board of Commissioners until 1810. Sadly, the physically imposing man who had relied on his charisma and stamina to lead men under trying conditions suffered a stroke in 1809. It partially paralyzed him. Later he fell into a fire and burned his leg severely enough to require amputation. Clark moved into a stately manor, Locust Grove, built by his sister and her husband, Revolutionary War veteran William Croghan. There he suffered another stroke and died in 1818.[11]

At the close of his life, George Rogers Clark's reputation was in tatters. There it remained until the end of the nineteenth century, when historians revisited his Revolutionary War campaigns and discovered in them a thrilling story: Clark and his hardy band of militia plunging into the wilderness to fight Native Americans and win the frontier for a new nation. It wasn't entirely true, but that first revision of Clark's history reflected the triumphalist and racist attitudes of the day. In rediscovering and rehabilitating Clark, the pendulum swung too far. By making excessive claims for his successes, particularly during the Illinois campaign, and declaring him a "conqueror," they invited a reaction and the pendulum swung again as the twenty-first century began. This second revision rightly dismissed the notion of Clark as a conqueror and instead focused on his explicit racism and the brutality of frontier warfare, almost as if they were the exclusive province of George Rogers Clark or his primary identifying characteristic.[12]

This second revision of Clark's reputation, however, downplays the sheer audacity of his military operations and their results. From the time of Clark's gunpowder mission at the end of 1776 through the middle of 1777, his diary recorded fourteen men killed and several more wounded and captured in Kentucky alone out of a total population under five hundred, more than two-thirds of whom were women and children, *before* Lieutenant Governor Hamilton took an active role supporting Native American raids. (Clark's count is not a comprehensive one.) In contrast, the Illinois campaign wrested the Illinois Country from Britain's weak grasp without killing anyone. Then, Clark held it in the face of a British counteroffensive. His victory at the Battle of Fort Sackville was nothing less than stunning. To be sure, Clark's execution of his Native American prisoners violated aspirational and evolving European laws of warfare, but it reflected the realities and brutality of frontier warfare, whether practiced by American, Frenchman, British, or Native American.

Clark thought in strategic terms grander than most of his frontier contemporaries. The new American nation was too weak to attack the British at Detroit, so Clark adopted an indirect approach, aiming for a chink in Britain's armor in Illinois. Although he overestimated the Illinois Country's role in sustaining British power in the West, Clark's thinking reflected a desire to seize the initiative. It served him well and he was able to combine that aggressiveness with an approach to the psychological battlefield that exploited divisions and uncertainties on the frontier. Simply, a cultivated reputation for strength and ruthlessness enabled him to build a base of power and influence in the Illinois Country that overcame Clark's failure to understand nuance among various Native American nations.

Clark was lucky in this respect. Had Native Americans been unified in support of Britain and in possession of greater information about the revolution, as Americans mistakenly believed they were, the Virginians along the Mississippi would have quickly failed. While Clark and his admirers believed he had cowed Native Americans into making peace, the truth was more complex. Instead, he introduced a new variable into the political dynamics among various groups north of the Ohio River. Tribes living in the area were as likely to use his presence to leverage better support from Britain as they were to give in to Clark's nurtured reputation for ruthlessness. For their part, French communities in the Illinois Country were also free to make the best deal possible for themselves with the Americans, British, Spanish, or even Native Americans as relative power balances shifted. Clark's decision to let them maintain large degrees of self-government and economic autonomy served his ends well by serving their needs. When Virginia lost interest in its claims in Illinois and failed to honor obligations incurred by Clark, local support for Clark and the Virginians naturally waned.

Clark's audacity played directly into his reading of his own men and the French population in the Illinois Country. Uncertain about their prospects on their own, Clark's seeming conviction and confidence of success could lead people to follow. Indeed, Clark's charisma seemed even to overcome the geography, weather, and ultimately, Lieutenant Governor Hamilton. The result was nothing short of astonishing. Britain had sought to use its Native American allies west of the Appalachians to destabilize thirteen coastal colonies. Instead, the Illinois campaign helped destabilize Britain's hold on its Trans-Appalachian frontier. Virginia earned a remarkable return for its modest investment in George Rogers Clark.

Notes

INTRODUCTION

1. Christian McMillen, "UVA and the History of Race: The George Rogers Clark Statute and Native Americans," *UVAToday*, July 27, 2020, https://news.virginia.edu/content/uva-and-history-race-george-rogers-clark-statue-and-native-americans.
2. Theodore Roosevelt, *The Winning of the West* (New York: G.P. Putnam's Sons, 1889), vol. 2.
3. William Hayden English, *Conquest of the Country Northwest of the River Ohio, 1778–1783 and Life of Gen. George Rogers Clark* (Indianapolis, IN: The Bowen-Merrill Company, 1897).
4. McMillen, "UVA and the History of Race."
5. Sanjay Suchak, "Photos: Removal of the George Rogers Clark Statue," *UVAToday*, July 21, 2021, https://news.virginia.edu/content/photos-removal-george-rogers-clark-statue. Clark's statue was removed along with those of his younger brother, the explorer William Clark, and the Confederate generals Robert E. Lee and Thomas Jonathan Jackson.

PROLOGUE

1. Attributed in a letter from Lord George Germain to Governor Carleton cited in John D. Barnhart, ed., *Henry Hamilton and George Rogers Clark in the American Revolution with The Unpublished Journal of Lieut. Gov. Henry Hamilton*, (Crawfordsville, IN: R.E. Banta, 1951), 28, and in Alan Fitzpatrick, *Wilderness War on the Ohio: The Untold Story of the Savage Battle for British and Indian Control of the Ohio Country During the American Revolution*, New Rev. 2nd ed. (Benwood, WV: Fort Henry Publications, 2005), 235–36. Barnhart disputes that this was Hamilton's intention and not simply Germain's idea being attributed Hamilton. In truth, many had suggested waging such a war, but its controversial nature made few eager to own it.
2. Germain's letter is available in Alan Fitzpatrick, *In their Own Words: Native American Voices from the American Revolution* (Benwood, WV: Fort Henry Publications, 2009), 57–58.
3. As in Europe, Indian Nations in North America evolved and changed over time. Many of these nations called the areas bordering the Great Lakes, from Ontario in Canada to

Ohio, Indiana, Illinois, Wisconsin, and Michigan in the United States. Rather than getting caught up in linguistic or geographically defined groups, however, the range of participants at Hamilton's Grand Council demonstrates the wide reach of Britain's influence among Native Americans.

4. "David Zeisberger to Col. George Morgan, July 7, 1777," Reuben Gold Thwaites and Louise Phelps Kellogg, eds., *Frontier Defense on the Upper Ohio, 1777–1778*, Draper Series, Volume III (Madison: Wisconsin Historical Society, 1912), 18–19. The rumors should be considered as such and reflect more the mindset on the frontier than matters of fact.

5. "Extract of Official Report of Hamilton," *Frontier Defense on the Upper Ohio, 1777–1778*, 7–14. The prior winter, a Chippewa Indian had killed an Ottawa Indian in Detroit. Hamilton paid the Ottawa in trade goods and wampum to ameliorate the loss and avoid the need for retribution.

6. Barnhart, *Henry Hamilton and George Rogers Clark*, 30.

7. "Hamilton's Proclamation," *Frontier Defense on the Upper Ohio*, 14.

CHAPTER ONE: EXCITING AN ALARM

1. William R. Nester, *George Rogers Clark* (Norman: University of Oklahoma Press, 2012), 4, 43; Lowell H. Harrison, *George Rogers Clark and the War in the West*, Kindle ed. (Lexington: The University Press of Kentucky, 1976), Loc. 118; Gwynne Tuell Potts, *George Rogers Clark and William Croghan* (Lexington: The University Press of Kentucky, 2020), 31–39.

2. The treaties had been signed with Indian nations elsewhere, notably the Iroquois and Cherokee, who claimed a form of suzerainty over Native Americans who lived west of the Appalachians, particularly in Ohio. Because tribes west of the Appalachians were increasingly willing to contest whatever authority they had conceded to the Iroquois in the past, many of their leaders also resented and rejected the treaties. Similarly, the American Revolution brought into question the legitimacy of the British and state authorities who had negotiated those treaties. For example, the Treaty of Sycamore Shoals was signed between the Transylvania Land Company and the Cherokee in a private transaction contested by the colony of Virginia. Exploring the nature of political authority on the frontier is not the subject of this book, but the lack of clarity created openings for increased conflict on the frontier.

3. Quoted in Temple Bodley, *George Rogers Clark: His Life and Public Services* (Boston, MA: Houghton Mifflin Company, 1926), 29.

4. Abraham Hite Jr., Clerk, "Petition from the Inhabitants of Kentucky, June 15, 1776" and "To the Honorable the Convention of Virginia, June 20, 1776," James Alton James, ed., *George Rogers Clark Papers, 1771–1781, Virginia Series, Volume III, Collections of the Illinois State Historical Library, Volume VIII* (Springfield: Illinois State Historical Library, 1912), 11–16.

5. "George Rogers Clark to John Brown, circa 1791," James, *George Rogers Clark Papers, 1771–1781*, 213. This lengthy letter later was the foundation for what became known as The Memoirs of George Rogers Clark. Although a more refined product was released as Clark's memoir, I will cite the letter because it was closer to Clark's voice and does not reflect the work of an editor. Future references will refer to this letter as the "Memoir." Henry appeared to be more receptive to Clark's overture than the council when it came to bringing Kentucky more clearly under Virginia's jurisdiction. After their conversation, Clark opted to only present the gunpowder petition, suggesting he and Henry discussed maneuvering

the council into consuming Kentucky in small bites. For the attitudes of Virginia's political leaders, see Jon Kukla, *Patrick Henry: Champion of Liberty* (New York: Simon and Schuster, 2017), 226–29.

6. "Petition by John Gabriel Jones and George Rogers Clark, October 1776," James, *George Rogers Clark Papers, 1771–1781*, 19.

7. Bob Drury and Tom Clavin, *Blood and Treasure: Daniel Boone and the Fight for America's First Frontier*, Kindle ed. (New York: St. Martin's Press, 2021), chapter 26.

8. Clark, "Memoir," *George Rogers Clark Papers, 1771–1781*, 14.

9. Ibid., 215.

10. Mark Edward Lender, "The Western Theater," in *Theaters of the American Revolution*, eds. James Kirby Martin and David L. Preston (Yardley, PA: Westholme Publishing, 2017).

11. Kevin J. Weddle, *The Compleat Victory: Saratoga and the American Revolution* (New York: Oxford University Press, 2021), 59, 62.

12. Andrew Jackson O'Shaughnessy, *The Men Who Lost America: British Leadership, the American Revolution, and the Fate of the Empire* (New Haven, CT: Yale University Press, 2013), 147.

13. "Letters of Lieut. Gov. Abbott to Gen. Carleton, June the 8th 1778," *Report of the Pioneer and Historical Society of the State of Michigan*, Vol. IX (Lansing, MI: Thorp & Godfrey, State Printers and Binders, 1886), 488–89.

14. Neal O. Hammon and Richard Taylor, *Virginia's Western War, 1775–1786* (Mechanicsburg, PA: Stackpole Books, 2002), 51–53.

15. "Clark's Diary," December 25, 1776, to January 2, 1778, James, *George Rogers Clark Papers, 1771–1781*, 22.

16. Ibid., 21–23.

17. Clark, "Memoir," *George Rogers Clark Papers, 1771–1781*, 216. Errors in original. Most of Clark's orders and correspondence contained better grammar and spelling, strongly suggesting portions of the memoir constituted notes and Clark had help composing other written products. The notes were likely those circulars that Hamilton had printed to be distributed across the frontier.

18. "To George Washington from Brigadier General Edward Hand, 15 September 1777," Founders Online, National Archives, https://founders.archives.gov/documents/Washington/03-11-02-0232.

19. "Col. John Bowman to Gen. Edward Hand, December 12th 1777," in *Frontier Defense on the Upper Ohio, 1777-1778*, Rueben Gold Thwaites, Louise Phelps Kellogg, eds., Draper Series, Volume III (Madison: Wisconsin Historical Society, 1912), 181.

20. "Letter of Henry Hamilton to Monsieur ? at the Illinois, circa Dec. 1777," Kathrine Wagner Seineke, *The George Rogers Clark Adventure in the Illinois* (New Orleans, LA: Polyanthos, 1981), 211–12. Seineke collected extensive primary documentation about the Illinois campaign in drafting her narrative history and published them along with it.

21. Hammon and Taylor, *Virginia's Western War, 1775–1786*, 51. The reorganization also included breaking off portions of Augusta County and forming three new counties in today's southwestern Pennsylvania, which also claimed the territory. So, for a time, Pennsylvania and Virginia had dual governments, dual courts, and dual militia systems attempting to assert control over the same land and people.

22. Ibid., 61.

23. "John Todd (1750–1782)," Kentucky Historical Society, https://apps.legislature.ky.gov/LegislativeMoments/moments09RS/web/Lincoln%20moments%2010.pdf. John Todd was killed at the Battle of Blue Licks near the end of the war.
24. Hammon and Taylor, *Virginia's Western War, 1775–1786*, 62–63.
25. Ibid., 53.

CHAPTER TWO: AN EXPEDITION OF GREAT CONSEQUENCE

1. For the definitive study of Dunmore's War, see Glenn F. Williams, *Dunmore's War: The Last Conflict of America's Colonial Era* (Yardley, PA: Westholme Publishing, 2017). Williams carefully and thoroughly examines the political maneuvering among various Indian nations and factions, the British, the colonies, and diverse economic interests leading up to the war, where he also examines Hokoleskwa's strategy and the Battle of Point Pleasant.
2. See Eric Sterner, "Chief Cornstalk's American Revolution, (part one)," *Emerging Revolutionary War Era*, April 18, 2018. Available at https://emergingrevolutionarywar.org/2018/04/18/155233/; Colin G. Calloway, *The Shawnees and the War for America* (New York: Viking, 2007), chapter 3.
3. Eric Sterner, "Chief Cornstalk's American Revolution (part two)," *Emerging Revolutionary War Era*, April 25, 2018. Available at: https://emergingrevolutionarywar.org/2018/04/25/chief-cornstalks-american-revolution-part-two/.
4. Clark, "Memoir," *George Rogers Clark Papers, 1771–1781*, 217.
5. "Clark to [Patrick Henry?], 1777," James, ed., *George Rogers Clark Papers, 1771–1781*, 21–22, 30–32.
6. "Clark's 'Diary,' December 25, 1776 to January 2, 1778," and "Clark to [Patrick Henry?], 1777," James, ed., *George Rogers Clark Papers, 1771–1781*, 21–22, 30–32. Clark's diary notes Linn and Moore's departure and return. The second document was transcribed from a damaged letter, parts of which were illegible. Historian Lyman Draper, who discovered the letter in the nineteenth century, concluded it was written in the summer/fall of 1777 and sent from Clark to Henry. The grammar is generally superior to other documents written by Clark, likely from the transcription; Nester, *George Rogers Clark*, 61.
7. Nester, *George Rogers Clark*, 61.
8. Clarence Walworth Alvord, ed., "Introduction," *Cahokia Records 1778–1790*, Collections of the Illinois State Historical Library, Volume II, Virginia Series, Vol. I (Springfield: Illinois State Historical Library, 1907), xxvii–xxxiii.
9. Clark, "Memoir," *George Rogers Clark Papers, 1771–1781*, 217.
10. Ibid., 218.
11. "George Rogers Clark to George Mason, November 19, 1779," James, *George Rogers Clark Papers, 1771–1781*, 115.
12. Henry Mayer, *A Son of Thunder: Patrick Henry and the American Republic*, Kindle ed. (New York: Grove Press, 1991), Loc. 4819-4858. If Lyman Draper's identification and dating of the Clark letter to Patrick Henry are accurate, the governor already knew of Clark's interest in invading Illinois.
13. Temple Bodley, *George Rogers Clark: His Life and Public Services* (Boston, MA: Houghton Mifflin Company, 1926), 43–44.
14. "Clark's 'Diary,' December 25, 1776 to January 2, 1778," James, *George Rogers Clark Papers, 1771–1781*, 27.

15. "Order of Council, January 2, 1778," and "Secret Instructions to Clark, January 2, 1778," James, *George Rogers Clark Papers, 1771–1781*, 33–36.

16. "Public Instructions to Clark, January 2, 1778" and "Secret Instructions to Clark, January 2, 1778," James, *George Rogers Clark Papers, 1771–1781*, 34–36.

17. "Letter of Patrick Henry to Bernardo De Galvez," 14 Jan., 1778," Seineke, *The George Rogers Clark Adventure in the Illinois*, 216–17.

18. "Patrick Henry to Clark, January 15, 1778," James, *George Rogers Clark Papers, 1771–1781*, 38.

19. "Secret Instructions to Clark, January 2, 1778," James, *George Rogers Clark Papers, 1771–1781*, 34–36.

20. "Patrick Henry to Edward Hand, January 2, 1778," James, *George Rogers Clark Papers, 1771–1781*, 36–37. The discrepancy in Clark's rank may have been an effort by Henry to conceal the expedition's purposes. Note: the mission's secrecy was in the process of being blown by James Willing. "Minutes of the Governor's Council of West Florida, 5th March, 1778," Michael J. Crawford, ed., *Naval Documents of the American Revolution, XI, American Theater: January 1, 1778–March 31, 1778, European Theater: January 1, 1778–March 31, 1778* (Washington, DC: Naval Historical Center, 2005), 521. Hereafter *NDAR*, volume, page.

21. "Wythe, Mason and Jefferson to Clark, January 3, 1778," "Patrick Henry to Edward Hand, January 2, 1778," James, *George Rogers Clark Papers, 1771–1781*, 37–38.

22. John E. Selby, *The Revolution in Virginia, 1775–1783* (Williamsburg, VA: The Colonial Williamsburg Foundation, 1988), 153–54.

23. Ibid., 190–91.

24. Duckworth, "Great Things Have Been Done by a Few Men," 28.

25. Nester, *George Rogers Clark*, 69.

26. "Patrick Henry to Clark, January 24, 1778," James, *George Rogers Clark Papers, 1771–1781*, 39.

27. "William Bailey Smith to Clark, March 7, 1778," James, *George Rogers Clark Papers, 1771–1781*, 39.

28. Harrison, *George Rogers Clark and the War in the West*, Loc. 319-329.

CHAPTER THREE: REBELS ON THE MISSISSIPPI: JAMES WILLING

1. Charles Rappleye, *Robert Morris: Financier of the American Revolution* (New York: Simon & Schuster, 2010), 216–17, 289.

2. Charles R. Smith, *Marines in the Revolution: A History of the Continental Marines in the American Revolution, 1775–1783* (Washington, DC: History and Museums Division, United States Marine Corps, 1975), 182.

3. "Colonel George Morgan to Captain James Willing, January 1778," *NDAR*, XI, 10.

4. Reuben Gold Thwaites and Louise Phelps Kellogg, eds., *Frontier Defense on the Upper Ohio, 1777–1778*, Draper Series, Volume III (Madison: Wisconsin Historical Society, 1912), Note 62, 191–92; See *NDAR*, XI, 6. The pay abstract and list of crewmen on the mission are on page 71 of this volume.

5. "Continental Commerce Committee to Robert Morris, February 21, 1778," *NDAR*, XI, 397–98.

6. Smith, *Marines in the Revolution*, 182; Edward Gay Mason, ed., *Philippe De Rocheblave and Rocheblave Papers* (Chicago, IL: Fergus Printing Company, 1890), 242. The Becquet

brothers were from Cahokia and Le Chance was from Kaskaskia, all on the Mississippi above the mouth of the Ohio. Thwaites and Kellogg, *Frontier Defense*, note 49, 286.

7. "Rocheblave to Carleton, 18 Fr. 1778," *Philippe De Rocheblave and Rocheblave Papers*, 273.

8. Jeff Dacus, "James Willing and the Mississippi Expedition," *Journal of the American Revolution*, April 18, 2019. Available at https://allthingsliberty.com/2019/04/james-willing-and-the-mississippi-expedition/.

9. "Minutes of the Governor's Council of West Florida, March 5th, 1778," *NDAR*, XI, 521–22.

10. Ibid., 522.

11. "Journal of Captain Mathew Phelps, February 21, 1778," *NDAR*, XI, 400.

12. Quoted in Smith, *Marines in the Revolution*, 184; "Minutes of the Governor's Council of West Florida, 10th March, 1778," *NDAR*, XI, 592.

13. Quoted in Smith, *Marines in the Revolution*, 185.

14. "Order of Captain James Willing, March 3, 1778," "Journal of Captain Mathew Phelps, February 21, 1778," *NDAR*, XI, 499.

15. "Colonel John Stuart to Lord George Germain, March 5 1778," *NDAR*, XI, 523–24.

16. "Minutes of the Governor's Council of West Florida, 2nd March 1778," *NDAR*, XI, 492.

17. Ibid., 490–91.

18. Smith, *Marines in the Revolution*, 186.

19. "Governor Don Bernardo De Galvez to Don Jose De Galvez, March 11, 1778," *NDAR*, XI, 607–8.

20. Smith, *Marines in the Revolution*, 186–87.

21. "Donald Campbell to Colonel John Stuart, March 20, 1778," *NDAR*, XI, 748.

22. "Governor Peter Chester to Brigadier General Augustine Prevost, 21st March 1778," *NDAR*, XI, 754.

23. Smith, *Marines in the Revolution*, 188.

24. "Petition of David Ross and Company to Don Bernardo De Galvez, April 11, 1778," Michael J. Crawford, ed., *Naval Documents of the American Revolution*, Volume 12 (Washington, DC: Naval History and Heritage Command, 2013), 93–94.

25. Smith, *Marines in the Revolution*, 188.

26. Ibid.

27. "Don Bernardo De Galvez, Governor of Louisiana, to William Smith and Robert Morris, May 5, 1778," *NDAR*, 12, 271.

28. "Oliver Pollock to the Continental Marine Committee, 7th May 1778," *NDAR*, 12, 286–89.

29. Smith, *Marines in the Revolution*, 190.

30. "Captain James Willing, Continental Army, to Oliver Pollock, 30th May 1778," *NDAR*, 12, 493.

31. "Oliver Pollock to Captain James Willing, Continental Army, 31st May, 1798," *NDAR*, 12, 502.

32. "Oliver Pollock to Don Bernardo De Galvez, Governor of Spanish Louisiana, 16th June, 1778," *NDAR*, 13, 130–31; Smith, *Marines in the Revolution*, 190.

33. Thomas E. Chavez, "St. Louis and the Trade that Helped Win United States Independence," in *The American Revolutionary War in the West*, ed. Stephen L. Kling Jr. (St.

Louis, MO: THGC Publishing, 2020), 21–25. The system developed by 1778 fell apart after the Illinois campaign as Virginia and the Continental Congress declined to honor bills incurred by Pollock and Clark for obtaining supplies.

CHAPTER FOUR: NO PART OF THE GLOBE: THE ILLINOIS COUNTRY

1. Duckworth, "Great Things Have Been Done by a Few Men," 2.

2. Thomas Hutchins, *A Topographical Description of Virginia, Pennsylvania, Maryland, and North Carolina Comprehending the Rivers Ohio, Kenhawa, Scioto, Cherokee, Wabash, Illinois, Mississippi, &c. The Climate Soil and Produce, Whether, Animal, Vegetable, Mineral; the Mountains, Creeks, Roads, Distances, Latitudes, &c. and of every Part, laid down in the annexed Map* (London: Printed for the Author, 1778), 13–14.

3. Nicholas Cresswell, *The Journal of Nicholas Cresswell, 1774–1777* (New York: The Dial Press, 1924), May 5 and 7, 1775 entries. Coming from Cresswell, who looked down on colonials, it was high praise indeed. Neither man knew of Lexington or Concord at that point.

4. M. J. Morgan, *Land of Big Rivers: French & Indian Illinois, 1699–1778* (Carbondale: Southern Illinois University Press, 2010).

5. David MacDonald and Raine Waters, *Kaskaskia: The Lost Capital of Illinois*, Kindle ed. (Carbondale: Southern Illinois University Press, 2019), 7.

6. Jacob F. Lee, *Masters of the Middle Waters: Indian Nations and Colonial Ambitions along the Mississippi* (Cambridge, MA: Harvard University Press, 2019), 109, 144.

7. Cathy Hellier, "Out of Adversity: The Smallpox Census," Colonial Williamsburg, May 1. 2020. Available at https://www.colonialwilliamsburg.org/learn/deep-dives/out-adversity-smallpox-census/; "In the Beginning: The Story of the Creation of the Nation's First Hospital," History of Pennsylvania Hospital, Penn Medicine. Available at https://www.uphs.upenn.edu/paharc/features/creation.html..

8. MacDonald and Waters, *Kaskaskia*, 24.

9. Ibid., 27; Lee, *Masters of the Middle Waters*, 154–55.

10. Captain Philip Pitman, *The Present State of the European Settlements on the Mississippi with a Geographical Description of that River* (London: Printed for J. Nourse, 1770), 42–43.

11. MacDonald and Waters, *Kaskaskia*, 32.

12. Ibid., 32; Clarence Edward Carter, *Great Britain and the Illinois Country, 1763–1774* (Washington, DC: The American Historical Association, 1910), 164.

13. Reuben Gold Thwaites and Louise Phelps Kellogg, eds., *Frontier Defense on the Upper Ohio, 1777–1778*, Draper Series, Volume III (Madison: Wisconsin Historical Society, 1912), note 30, 10.

14. Mason, notes and sketches, *Philippe de Rocheblave and Rocheblave Papers*, 233–34.

15. Mason, *Philippe de Rocheblave and Rocheblave Papers*, 237.

16. "Petition to Carleton concerning Rocheblave, 10th April, 1777," Mason, *Philippe de Rocheblave and Rocheblave Papers*, 256. Originals in *"Canadian Archives," Haldimand Papers*, Series B., Vol. 185, I, 2. Thomas Bentley was the only petitioner willing to sign the document. Rocheblave retaliated by accusing him of rebellious sympathies. The commandant at Mackinac arrested Bentley, who was then sent to Montreal and jailed for two years. He escaped to Williamsburg in November 1779, proclaimed his loyalty to the American cause, later made his way to Vincennes on the Wabash, where he proclaimed his loyalty to the

British side, and then turned up in Richmond in 1781, seeking compensation for property seized by the British! Clearly, the London-born merchant was a man looking to his own ends and willing to play both sides. Clark, however, trusted him and Bentley successfully established land claims at Kaskaskia. Mason, note, *Philippe de Rocheblave and Rocheblave Papers*, 259–60.

17. "Rocheblave to Lieut.-Gov. Hamilton, 8th May, 1777," Mason, *Philippe de Rocheblave and Rocheblave Papers*, 262–63. Originals in "Canadian Archives," Series Q, Vol. 14, 64.

CHAPTER FIVE: CLARK ADVANCES

1. John Bakeless, *Background to Glory: The Life of George Rogers Clark*, reprint (Lincoln: University of Nebraska Press, 1992), 56.

2. "Clark's Memoir," James, *George Rogers Clark Papers, 1771–1781*, 221.

3. Ibid., 221.

4. Nester, *George Rogers Clark: "I Glory in War"* (Norman: University of Oklahoma Press, 2012), 72.

5. Lowell Harrison, *George Rogers Clark and the War in the West*, Kindle ed. (Lexington: The University Press of Kentucky, 1976), 20.

6. "Clark's Memoir," James, *George Rogers Clark Papers, 1771–1781*, 222. Decades later, two cement companies mined Clark Island for rock while engineers altered the river to control flooding and facilitate navigation. Consequently, Corn Island no longer exists. John W. Wayland, *The Bowmans: A Pioneering Family in Virginia, Kentucky and the Northwest Territory* (Staunton, VA: The McClure Company, Inc., 1943), 73.

7. Duckworth, "Great Things Have Been Done by a Few Men," 29.

8. "Clark's Memoir," James, *George Rogers Clark Papers, 1771–1781*, 222.

9. Ibid., 222.

10. Bakeless, *Background to Glory*, 58; Nester, *George Rogers Clark*, 72–73; "George Rogers Clark to George Mason, November 19, 1779," James, *George Rogers Clark Papers, 1771–1781*, 118. Clark spelled the lieutenant's name "Hutchings."

11. "Clark's Memoir," James, *George Rogers Clark Papers, 1771–1781*, 223; "George Rogers Clark to George Mason, November 19, 1779," James, *George Rogers Clark Papers, 1771–1781*, 118.

12. "Clark's Memoir," James, *George Rogers Clark Papers, 1771–1781*, 223; "George Rogers Clark to George Mason, November 19, 1779," James, *George Rogers Clark Papers, 1771–1781*, 118; Nester, *George Rogers Clark*, 72.

13. Nester, *George Rogers Clark*, 72.

14. Duckworth, "Great Things Have Been Done by a Few Men," 30; Wayland, *The Bowmans*, 73; "Clark's Memoir" James, *George Rogers Clark Papers, 1771–1781*, 224.

15. "Clark's Memoi,r" James, *George Rogers Clark Papers, 1771–1781*, 224.

16. Ibid., 226.

17. "Clark's Memoir," James, *George Rogers Clark Papers, 1771–1781*, 225–26; Harrison, *George Rogers Clark and the War in the West*, 22.

18. Quoted in Temple Bodley, *George Rogers Clark: His Life and Public Services* (Boston, MA: Houghton Mifflin Company, 1926), 61.

19. "George Rogers Clark to George Mason, November 19, 1779," James, *George Rogers Clark Papers, 1771-1781*, 119.

20. "Clark's Memoir," James, *George Rogers Clark Papers, 1771-1781*, 226–27.

21. Wayland, *The Bowmans*, 73–74.

CHAPTER SIX: KASKASKIA FALLS

1. "Letter of Lieut. Governor Hamilton to General Carleton, April 25th, 1779," Seineke, *The George Rogers Clark Adventure in the Illinois*, 235.

2. Wampum were a kind of bead that could be woven into a belt in various colors and symbols that communicated a message and were a popular form of formal diplomatic communication.

3. "Hamilton to McKee" and "Gov. Henry Hamilton to Sir Guy Carleton, 25 April 1778," Reuben Gold Thwaites and Louise Phelps Kellogg, eds., *Frontier Defense on the Upper Ohio, 1777–1778*, Draper Series, Volume III (Madison: Wisconsin Historical Society, 1912), 274, 280–88; Seineke, *The George Rogers Clark Adventure in the Illinois*, 235.

4. "Rocheblave to Lord George Germain, 28th February, 1778," Moses, ed., *Philippe De Rocheblave and Rocheblave Papers*, 278. One might read this as Rocheblave asking for a more senior replacement, but it is more likely Rocheblave hoped to be promoted into the role of lieutenant governor at Kaskaskia.

5. "Rocheblave to Carleton (?), July 4, 1778," Moses, *Philippe De Rocheblave and Rocheblave Papers*, 287–88.

6. Duckworth, "Great Things Have Been Done by a Few Good Men: Operational Art in Clark's Illinois Campaign of 1778–1779," 30.

7. "Clark's Memoir," James, *George Rogers Clark Papers, 1771–1781*, 227; "George Rogers Clark to George Mason, November 19, 1779," James, *George Rogers Clark Papers, 1771–1781*, 120.

8. "Clark's Memoir," James, *George Rogers Clark Papers, 1771–1781*, 228.

9. "Letter of Don Fernando De Leyba to Bernardo De Galvez at New Orleans, 11 July 1778," Seineke, *The George Rogers Clark Adventure in the Illinois*, 262–63. In translation, De Leyba describes the "ruckus" as a "riot," but the lack of bloodshed and Clark's prepositioning of his troops suggests more in the way of chaos or confusion quickly brought under control.

10. Harrison, *George Rogers Clark and the War in the West*, Kindle ed., 23–24.

11. Harrison, *George Rogers Clark and the War in the West*, Kindle ed., 24. The town's population at any given moment could only be estimated. Records were imperfect, and people arrived and departed at will as the hunting, trapping, and trading seasons passed every year. So, population figures should be taken with a grain of salt.

12. "Clark's Memoir," James, *George Rogers Clark Papers, 1771–1781*, 229.

13. Joseph P. Donnelly, *Pierre Gibault: Missionary, 1737–1802* (Chicago: Loyola University Press, 1971).

14. "Clark's Memoir," James, *George Rogers Clark Papers, 1771–1781*, 229–30.

15. Ibid., 230.

16. Brady Crytzer, *War in the Peaceable Kingdom: The Kittanning Raid of 1756* (Yardley, PA: Westholme Publishing, 2016), 137–49.

17. "Clark's Memoir," James, *George Rogers Clark Papers, 1771–1781*, 230; William R. Nester, *George Rogers Clark* (Norman: University of Oklahoma Press, 2012), 79.

CHAPTER SEVEN: SEIZING THE REST OF THE ILLINOIS COUNTRY

1. "Clark's Memoir," James, *George Rogers Clark Papers, 1771–1781*, 232.

2. Harrison, *George Rogers Clark and the War in the West*, Loc. 434.

3. "Clark's Memoir," James, *George Rogers Clark Papers, 1771–1781*, 232.

4. John Wayland, *The Bowmans: A Pioneering Family in Virginia, Kentucky, and the Northwest Territory* (Staunton, VA: The McClure Company, Inc., 1943), 27–28.

5. Ibid., 33.

6. Ibid., 45.

7. "Clark's Memoir," James, *George Rogers Clark Papers, 1771–1781*, 232. Bowman was a captain at this point, but Cark referred to him in his memoir by a rank Bowman later received.

8. "Clark's Memoir," James, *George Rogers Clark Papers, 1771–1781*, 233.

9. Harrison, *George Rogers Clark and the War in the West*, Kindle ed., 27.

10. "Clark's Memoir," James, *George Rogers Clark Papers, 1771–1781*, 233.

11. Harrison, *George Rogers Clark and the War in the West*, Kindle ed., 28.

12. Wayland, *The Bowmans*, 76. Wayland includes a letter from Bowman to his uncle, Colonel John Hite in his text.

13. Harrison, *George Rogers Clark and the War in the West*, 27.

14. Nester, *George Rogers Clark*, 81.

15. "Clark's Memoir," James, *George Rogers Clark Papers, 1771–1781*, 238.

16. Nester, *George Rogers Clark*, 81; "Clark's Memoir," James, *George Rogers Clark Papers, 1771-1781*, 238; Donnelly, *Pierre Gibault: Missionary, 1737–1802*, 71–72; "Clark to Jean B. Laffont, July 14, 1778," James, *George Rogers Clark Papers, 1771–1781*, 53–54.

17. "Clark to Inhabitants of Vincennes, July [13?], 1778," James, *George Rogers Clark Papers, 1771–1781*, 51.

18. Ibid., 52.

19. "Oath of Inhabitants of Vincennes, July 20, 1778," James, *George Rogers Clark Papers, 1771–1781*, 56–59.

20. Donnelly, *Pierre Gibault: Missionary, 1737–1802*, 73.

CHAPTER EIGHT: SECURING AMERICAN GAINS

1. "Gabriel Cerre to Clark, July 11, 1778," James, *George Rogers Clark Papers, 1771–1781*, 47–49.

2. Nester, *George Rogers Clark*, 82; Harrison, *George Rogers Clark and the War in the West*, Kindle ed., 29–30.

3. Morgan, *Land of Big Rivers: French & Indian Illinois, 1699–1778*, Kindle ed., Loc. 2144-2153 of 3994.

4. Clarence Edwin Carter, *Great Britain and the Illinois Country, 1763–1774* (Washington, DC: The American Historical Association, 1910), 96.

5. Nester, *George Rogers Clark*, 83.

6. Robert Michael Morrissey, *Empire by Collaboration: Indians, Colonists, and Governments in Colonial Illinois Country* (Philadelphia: University of Pennsylvania Press, 2015), 232–33. Morrissey's book is an excellent examination of how British neglect of the Illinois Country hampered development of the communities there and exacerbated conflicts among groups living in the region by allowing them to fester. Despite Clark's skills as a psychological war-

rior, he did not comprehend these complexities. But he did not need to in order to exploit the resulting uncertainty for his own ends.

7. Morgan, *Land of Big Rivers: French & Indian Illinois, 1699–1778*, Kindle ed., Loc. 2169 of 3994; Carter, *Great Britain and the Illinois Country, 1763-1774*, 81–84.

8. "Clark's Memoir," James, *George Rogers Clark Papers, 1771–1781*, 243.

9. Ibid., 243.

10. Ibid., 244–45. Parentheticals in original.

11. Ibid., 245.

12. Ibid., 245–46.

13. Ibid., 247.

14. Morrissey, *Empire by Collaboration*, 233.

15. "Clark's Memoir," James, *George Rogers Clark Papers, 1771–1781*, 249; Harrison, *George Rogers Clark and the War in the West*, Loc. 514; Nester, *George Rogers Clark*, 84–85. The Winnebago are today more generally known as the Ho-Chunk. The name, "Winnebago" may have its origins with the Potowatomi, whose name itself may have been learned by whites from the Ojibwe, known to whites as the Chippewa.

16. "Clark's Memoir," James, *George Rogers Clark Papers, 1771–1781*, 251–52.

17. Ibid., 252.

18. Ibid., 254.

19. Michael A. McDonnell, *Masters of Empire: Great Lakes Indians and the Making of America*, Kindle ed. (New York: Hill and Wang, 2015), chapter 7.

20. Andrew J. Blackbird, *History of the Ottawa and Chippewa Indians of Michigan: A Grammar of Their Language, and Personal and Family History of the Author* (Ypsilanti, MI: The Ypsilantian Job Printing House, 1887), 8–9.

21. McDonnell, *Masters of Empire: Great Lakes Indians and the Making of America*, Kindle ed., 284.

22. Richard White, *The Middle Ground: Indians, Empires, and Republics in the Great Lakes Region, 1650–1814,* 20th Anniversary Edition (New York: Cambridge University Press, 2011), 170–71; Harrison, *George Rogers Clark and the War in the West*, Kindle ed., 31–32; Nester, *George Rogers Clark,* 86–87.

23. McDonnell, *Masters of the Empire: Great Lakes Indians and the Making of America*, Kindle ed., 290–91.

24. "John Bowman to Clark, October 14, 1778," James, *George Rogers Clark Papers, 1771–1781*, 70.

25. Duckworth, "Great Things Have Been Done by a Few Men," 34.

26. "Clark's Memoir," James, *George Rogers Clark Papers, 1771–1781*, 241.

27. Harrison, *George Rogers Clark and the War in the West*, 34–35; Nester, *George Rogers Clark,* 93–94. Rocheblave's behavior enabled Clark to justify seizing his property and slaves, which he could then sell off to distribute the proceeds among his men.

28. Duckworth, "Great Things Have Been Done by a Few Men," 35; Harrison, *George Rogers Clark and the War in the West*, Loc. 557-571.

CHAPTER NINE: HAMILTON'S COUNTEROFFENSIVE

1. "Rocheblave to Carleton, April [August] 3, 1778," Moses, *Philippe De Rocheblave and Rocheblave Papers*, 289–90.

2. "Letter of Lieut. Governor Hamilton to General Carleton: Received by Haldimand, 11 Aug. 1778," Seineke, *The George Rogers Clark Adventure in the Illinois*, 270–71.

3. "Summary of Hamilton's Report on Two Indian Councils, 14 June–3 July, 1778," Seineke, *The George Rogers Clark Adventure in the Illinois*, 248.

4. Harrison, *George Rogers Clark and the War in the West*, Kindle ed., 39–40.

5. John D. Barnhart, ed., *Henry Hamilton and George Rogers Clark in the American Revolution* (Crawfordsville, IN: R.E. Banta, 1951), 14–15. Barnhart is the author of a short Hamilton biography and editor of Hamilton's journal, included in the volume.

6. Quoted in Barnhart, *Henry Hamilton and George Rogers Clark in the American Revolution*, 11.

7. "Letter of General Haldimand to Lieut. Governor Hamilton, 27th August 1778," Seineke, *The George Rogers Clark Adventure in the Illinois*, 276–77. Of course, these were always possibilities, but not ones Hamilton had heretofore developed.

8. William L. Potter, *Redcoats on the Frontier: A Study of the King's 8th Regiment in North America*, self-published, 2023, 104–5. Potter's work is an updated and edited version of his 1988 master's thesis at Murray State University.

9. Barnhart, *Henry Hamilton and George Rogers Clark in the American Revolution with the Unpublished Journal of Lieut. Gov. Henry Hamilton*, 103–4.

10. "Account of the Expedition of Lieut. Gov. Hamilton," *Report of the Pioneer and Historical Society of the State of Michigan*, Vol. IX, 492. Hamilton composed this account in July 1781 in the form of a letter to his superiors. See also, Harrison, *George Rogers Clark and the War in the West*, 40. Harrison allows for some estimation in the final numbers. A rough approximation is more useful than Hamilton's more precise recollection because men came and went from the amalgamation of the Anglo/Franco/Indian force as various individuals were dispatched and arrived from specific tasks, such as scouting, delivering messages, etc.

11. Normand MacLeod, *Detroit to Fort Sackville, 1778–1779: The Journal of Normand MacLeod* (Detroit, MI: Wayne State University Press, 1978), xi–xii. Hamilton laid out a slightly different load in his journal, but the same total weight. Barnhart, *Henry Hamilton and George Rogers Clark in the American Revolution with the Unpublished Journal of Lieut. Gov. Henry Hamilton*, 104.

12. MacLeod's biography comes from Evans' introduction in MacLeod, *Detroit to Fort Sackville, 1778–1779*. Hamilton did not have the authority to make MacLeod's appointment and the matter became a problem after Hamilton's capture.

13. MacLeod, *Detroit to Fort Sackville, 1778–1779*, 15.

14. Ibid., 20.

15. Ibid., 24.

16. Ibid., 32–33.

17. Ibid., 34–35.

18. Nester, *George Rogers Clark*, 106; Harrison, *George Rogers Clark and the War in the West*, Kindle ed., 40.

19. Barnhart, *Henry Hamilton and George Rogers Clark in the American Revolution*, 107.

20. MacLeod, *Detroit to Fort Sackville, 1778–1779*, 66–67; Barnhart, *Henry Hamilton and George Rogers Clark in the American Revolution*, 114–15.

21. Barnhart, *Henry Hamilton and George Rogers Clark in the American Revolution*, 115.

CHAPTER TEN: HAMILTON ON THE WABASH

1. Barnhart, *Henry Hamilton and George Rogers Clark in the American Revolution with the Unpublished Journal of Lieut. Gov. Henry Hamilton*, 117.

2. Ibid., 118.

3. MacLeod, *Detroit to Fort Sackville, 1778–1779*, 76.

4. Harrison, *George Rogers Clark and the War in the West*, 41.

5. Barnhart, *Henry Hamilton and George Rogers Clark in the American Revolution*, 126; MacLeod, *Detroit to Fort Sackville, 1778–1779*, 85.

6. Barnhart, *Henry Hamilton and George Rogers Clark in the American Revolution*, 132.

7. Harrison, *George Rogers Clark and the War in the West*, 44.

8. Barnhart, *Henry Hamilton and George Rogers Clark in the American Revolution*, 139; MacLeod, *Detroit to Fort Sackville, 1778–1779*, 95.

9. Ibid., 140; Ibid., 96–97.

10. Ibid., 146; Ibid., 108.

11. Ibid., 146–47; Ibid., 110.

12. "Leonard Helm to Clark, December 17,1778," James, *George Rogers Clark Papers, 1771–1781*, 89–90.

13. Barnhart, *Henry Hamilton and George Rogers Clark in the American Revolution*, 146–47; "Letter of Lieut. Governor Hamilton to General Haldimand, Dec. 18th 1778," Seineke, *The George Rogers Clark Adventure in the Illinois*, 333–34.

14. Barnhart, ed., *Henry Hamilton and George Rogers Clark in the American Revolution*, 148.

15. Ibid., 148–49; MacLeod, *Detroit to Fort Sackville, 1778–1779*, 112.

16. Barnhart, *Henry Hamilton and George Rogers Clark in the American Revolution*, 149.

17. Ibid., 150; Nester, *George Rogers Clark*, 112–13.

18. Barnhart, *Henry Hamilton and George Rogers Clark in the American Revolution*, 161.

19. Ibid., 153. Old Tobacco, of course, did not discuss internal tribal politics with the lieutenant governor either.

20. Ibid., 154.

21. Harrison, *George Rogers Clark and the War in the West*, Kindle ed., 44.

CHAPTER ELEVEN: AN ALARM IN KASKASKIA

1. "Clark's Memoir," James, ed., *George Rogers Clark Papers, 1771–1781*, 259.

2. Ibid., 261.

3. "Clark's Memoir," James, ed., *George Rogers Clark Papers, 1771–1781*, 262; "George Rogers Clark to George Mason, November 19, 1779," James, George Rogers Clark Papers, 1771-1781, 132-133.

4. "Clark's Memoir," James, ed., *George Rogers Clark Papers, 1771–1781*, 262.

5. Ibid., 265. Clark speculated that the Indians who spotted him were a small observation party of a larger group.

6. Ibid., 262. The Indians who had spotted Clark and his men laughing at the poor man attempting to transport furniture on the road from Kaskaskia earlier in the day may have been part of this larger group.

7. Ibid., 263.

8. Ibid., 263.

9. Ibid., 264.

10. Ibid.
11. Ibid., 264.
12. Ibid., 264–65.
13. Ibid., 266.

CHAPTER TWELVE: A FEW MEN WELL CONDUCTED

1. Nester, *George Rogers Clark*, 88–89.
2. Ibid., 113.
3. Kristine L. Sjostrom, "Fernando de Leyba: Defender of St. Louis," in *The American Revolutionary War in the West*, ed. Stephen L. Kling Jr. (St. Louis, MO: THGC Publishing, 2020), 133–34.
4. Bruno Roselli, *Vigo: A Forgotten Builder of the American Republic* (Boston, MA: The Stratford Company, 1933), 43–57. The economic situation on the Spanish side of the river was challenging as more citizens were shifting from farming to trade, leading to risks of food shortages. Sjostrom, "Fernando de Leyba," 137–38, Clark's arrival exacerbated the difficulties.
5. Roselli, *Vigo*, 70–71. Roselli has a tendency to wax poetic about the subjects of his biography. He takes to task historians who dismiss the romantic interest hypothesis of Clark's interest in the de Leyba family as unsupported by evidence, but offers no real evidence for it, either.
6. "Clark's Memoir," James, ed., *George Rogers Clark Papers, 1771–1781*, 267.
7. Ibid., 267. Clark's explanation of the situation may have benefitted from hindsight in his memoir, which was roughed out well after Hamilton's capture. But it is not inconsistent with his own view of the positional advantages he hoped to gain by capturing the Illinois Country in 1777. So, we can give him the benefit of the doubt.
8. Ibid., 267.
9. "Letter of G.R. Clark to Patrick Henry Feby 3d 1779," in Seineke, *The George Rogers Clark Adventure*, 348.
10. "Clark's Memoir," James, ed., *George Rogers Clark Papers, 1771–1781*, 268.
11. Henry Pirtle, ed., *Col. George Rogers Clark's Sketch of his Campaign in the Illinois in 1778-9 . . . and Major Bowman's Journal of the Taking of Post St. Vincent's* (Cincinnati, OH: Roberg Clarke & Co., 1869), 99. Hereafter "*Major Bowman's Journal.*"
12. "Clark's Memoir," James, ed., *George Rogers Clark Papers, 1771–1781*, 269.
13. Harrison, *George Rogers Clark and the War in the West*, Loc. 722.
14. "Letter of Instructions from G.R. Clark to Lieut John Rogers, Feb'y 3d, 1779," in Seineke, *The George Rogers Clark Adventure*, 349.
15. "Letter of G.R. Clark to Patrick Henry Feby 3d 1779," in Seineke, *The George Rogers Clark Adventure*, 349.
16. "Major Bowman's Journal," in Pirtle, *Col. George Rogers Clark's Sketch of his Campaign in the Illinois in 1778–1779*, 100; "Clark's Memoir," James, *George Rogers Clark Papers, 1771–1781*, 269.
17. Barnhart, *Henry Hamilton and George Rogers Clark in the American Revolution with the Unpublished Journal of Lieut. Gov. Henry Hamilton*, 173–74.
18. Ibid., 174.

19. "Clark's Memoir," James, ed., *George Rogers Clark Papers, 1771–1781*, 269; "Major Bowman's Journal," in Pirtle, ed., *Col. George Rogers Clark's Sketch of his Campaign in the Illinois in 1778–1779*, 100.

20. "Clark's Memoir," James, ed., *George Rogers Clark Papers, 1771–1781*, 269–70.

21. Ibid., 270.

22. Ibid..

23. Barnhart, *Henry Hamilton and George Rogers Clark in the American Revolution*, 174.

24. "Clark's Memoir," James, ed., *George Rogers Clark Papers, 1771–1781*, 270; "Major Bowman's Journal," in Pirtle, ed., *Col. George Rogers Clark's Sketch of his Campaign in the Illinois in 1778–1779*, 100.

25. "Clark's Memoir," James, ed., *George Rogers Clark Papers, 1771–1781*, 271.

26. "Major Bowman's Journal," in Pirtle, ed., *Col. George Rogers Clark's Sketch of his Campaign in the Illinois in 1778–1779*, 101.

27. "Clark's Memoir," James, ed., *George Rogers Clark Papers, 1771–1781*, 271.

28. "Major Bowman's Journal," in Pirtle, ed., *Col. George Rogers Clark's Sketch of his Campaign in the Illinois in 1778–1779*, 101; "Clark's Memoir," James, ed., *George Rogers Clark Papers, 1771–1781*, 271.

29. "Clark's Memoir," James, ed., *George Rogers Clark Papers, 1771–1781*, 272.

30. "Major Bowman's Journal," in Pirtle, ed., *Col. George Rogers Clark's Sketch of his Campaign in the Illinois in 1778–1779*, 101.

31. Barnhart, *Henry Hamilton and George Rogers Clark in the American Revolution*, 175.

32. "Major Bowman's Journal," in Pirtle, ed., *Col. George Rogers Clark's Sketch of his Campaign in the Illinois in 1778–1779*, 102.

33. Ibid., 102.

34. "Clark's Memoir," James, ed., *George Rogers Clark Papers, 1771–1781*, 273.

35. "Major Bowman's Journal," in Pirtle, ed., *Col. George Rogers Clark's Sketch of his Campaign in the Illinois in 1778–1779*, 102.

36. Barnhart, *Henry Hamilton and George Rogers Clark in the American Revolution*, 175.

37. Ibid.

38. "Major Bowman's Journal," in Pirtle, ed., *Col. George Rogers Clark's Sketch of his Campaign in the Illinois in 1778–1779*, 102. Bowman gave the number as two canoes, likely the one Captain McCarty had used and the one recovered on the Wabash. This leaves open the fate of the pirogue completed on March 14 and used to ferry baggage and ill men through the water since then. Pirogues could be quite heavy, and Clark's men had likely found enough dry ground to march on so as to require its abandonment. It also begs the disposition of the third boat full of locals that had come in the day before. Clark still had them with him on the twenty-second.

39. "Clark's Memoir," James, ed., *George Rogers Clark Papers, 1771–1781*, 273, n1.

40. Ibid., 273; "Major Bowman's Journal," in Pirtle, ed., *Col. George Rogers Clark's Sketch of his Campaign in the Illinois in 1778–1779*, 102–3. Bowman referred to the Mamel as Momib or Bubbriss.

41. Harrison, *George Rogers Clark and the War in the West*, Loc. 793; "Major Bowman's Journal," in Pirtle, ed., *Col. George Rogers Clark's Sketch of his Campaign in the Illinois in 1778–1779*, 102–3.

42. "Clark's Memoir," James, ed., *George Rogers Clark Papers, 1771–1781*, 274.

43. Ibid., 274.

44. Ibid.

45. "Major Bowman's Journal," in Pirtle, ed., *Col. George Rogers Clark's Sketch of his Campaign in the Illinois in 1778–1779*, 103.

46. McDonnell, *Masters of Empire*, 290.

47. Barnhart, *Henry Hamilton and George Rogers Clark in the American Revolution with the Unpublished Journal of Lieut. Gov. Henry Hamilton*, 177–78.

48. "Clark's Memoir," James, ed., *George Rogers Clark Papers, 1771–1781*, 275.

49. "Major Bowman's Journal," in Pirtle, *Col. George Rogers Clark's Sketch of his Campaign in the Illinois in 1778–1779*, 104.

50. "Clark's Memoir," James, ed., *George Rogers Clark Papers, 1771–1781*, 275, "Major Bowman's Journal," in Pirtle, *Col. George Rogers Clark's Sketch of his Campaign in the Illinois in 1778–1779*, 104.

51. "Clark's Memoir," James, ed., *George Rogers Clark Papers, 1771–1781*, 276.

52. "Clark's Memoir," James, ed., *George Rogers Clark Papers, 1771–1781*, 276–77.

CHAPTER THIRTEEN: OPENING MOVES IN THE BATTLE FOR FORT SACKVILLE

1. Clark places the town half a league away from the fort in his letter to Mason, but his declaration to the town in his memoir announces his army is two miles away from the town and fort.

2. "Clark's Memoir," James, ed., *George Rogers Clark Papers, 1771–1781*, 276–77; "George Rogers Clark to George Mason," James, ed., *George Rogers Clark Papers, 1771–1781*, 141; "Major Bowman's Journal," in Pirtle, ed., *Col. George Rogers Clark's Sketch of his Campaign in the Illinois in 1778–1779*, 104.

3. "Clark's Memoir," James, ed., *George Rogers Clark Papers, 1771–1781*, 277.

4. "Clark to George Mason," James, ed., *George Rogers Clark Papers, 1771–1781*, 141.

5. "Clark's Memoir," James, ed., *George Rogers Clark Papers, 1771–1781*, 277.

6. Ibid., 277–78.

7. Ibid., 278, 280.

8. "Clark to George Mason," James, ed., *George Rogers Clark Papers, 1771–1778*, 165.

9. "Clark's Memoir," James, ed., *George Rogers Clark Papers, 1771–1781*, 279.

10. Ibid.; "Major Bowman's Journal," in Pirtle, ed., *Col. George Rogers Clark's Sketch of his Campaign in the Illinois in 1778–1779*, 104.

11. Barnhart, *Henry Hamilton and George Rogers Clark in the American Revolution with the Unpublished Journal of Lieut. Gov. Henry Hamilton*, 178.

CHAPTER FOURTEEN: GREAT THINGS HAVE BEEN ACCOMPLISHED

1. Harrison, *George Rogers Clark and the War in the West*, Loc. 859; "Clark's Memoir," James, ed., *George Rogers Clark Papers, 1771–1781*, 283.

2. "Clark's Memoir," James, ed., *George Rogers Clark Papers, 1771–1781*, 280; "Major Bowman's Journal," in Pirtle, ed., *Col. George Rogers Clark's Sketch of his Campaign in the Illinois in 1778–1779*, 105; Barnhart, *Henry Hamilton and George Rogers Clark in the American Revolution with the Unpublished Journal of Lieut. Gov. Henry Hamilton*, 178–79.

3. Barnhart, *Henry Hamilton and George Rogers Clark in the American Revolution*, 178–79.

4. "Clark's Memoir," James, ed., *George Rogers Clark Papers, 1771–1781*, 283–84.

5. Ibid., 282–83.

6. Ibid.

7. Barnhart, *Henry Hamilton and George Rogers Clark in the American Revolution*, 178–79.

8. "Clark's Memoir," James, ed., *George Rogers Clark Papers, 1771–1781*, 283.

9. Ibid. Hamilton understandably blamed Clark for the partial scalping, claiming the Virginian had ordered it done until Maisonville's brother, who was fighting on Clark's side, intervened. Barnhart, *Henry Hamilton and George Rogers Clark in the American Revolution*, 182.

10. Harrison, *George Rogers Clark and the War in the West*, 56.

11. Clark refers to this Piankeshaw leader as Big Tobacco. Whether it was Old Tobacco or his son, Young Tobacco, is unclear.

12. "Clark's Memoir," James, ed., *George Rogers Clark Papers, 1771–1781*, 281; "Major Bowman's Journal," in Pirtle, ed., *Col. George Rogers Clark's Sketch of his Campaign in the Illinois in 1778–1779*, 105.

13. "Clark's Memoir," James, ed., *George Rogers Clark Papers, 1771–1781*, 282; "Major Bowman's Journal," in Pirtle, ed., *Col. George Rogers Clark's Sketch of his Campaign in the Illinois in 1778–1779*, 105; Barnhart, *Henry Hamilton and George Rogers Clark in the American Revolution*, 179–80.

14. Barnhart, *Henry Hamilton and George Rogers Clark in the American Revolution*, 177; "Clark's Memoir," James, ed., *George Rogers Clark Papers, 1771–1781*, 285.

15. "Clark's Memoir," James, ed., *George Rogers Clark Papers, 1771–1781*, 285. "Them" referred to the papers taken off Hamilton's prisoners, which were useless, and supplies within the fort. Hamilton's record of Clark's note outlined it as a demand for immediate surrender of the garrison, prisoners, papers, stores, and fort and a threat to expect no mercy in the event of resistance sent at 11:00 a.m. Bowman recorded something similar sent about 9:00 a.m. Clark informed George Mason of Virginia that he sent the note around 8:00 a.m. Barnhart, *Henry Hamilton and George Rogers Clark in the American Revolution*, 180; "Major Bowman's Journal," in Pirtle, ed., *Col. George Rogers Clark's Sketch of his Campaign in the Illinois in 1778–1779*, 105–6.

16. Harrison, *George Rogers Clark and the War in the West*, Loc. 863.

17. Barnhart, *Henry Hamilton and George Rogers Clark in the American Revolution*, 181.

18. "Clark's Memoir," James, ed., *George Rogers Clark Papers, 1771–1781*, 285.

19. "Major Bowman's Journal," in Pirtle, ed., *Col. George Rogers Clark's Sketch of his Campaign in the Illinois in 1778–1779*, 105–6.

20. "Clark's Memoir," James, ed., *George Rogers Clark Papers, 1771–1781*, 288; Barnhart, *Henry Hamilton and George Rogers Clark in the American Revolution*, 181; "Major Bowman's Journal," in Pirtle, ed., *Col. George Rogers Clark's Sketch of his Campaign in the Illinois in 1778–1779*, 107. Clark counted fifteen captured or killed and the rescue of two prisoners, based in part on his later information that only one warrior returned to his home; Hamilton claimed one dead, two wounded, and five captured; Bowman recorded two dead, three wounded, and six captured.

21. "George Rogers Clark to George Mason, November 19, 1779," James, ed., *George Rogers Clark Papers, 1771-1781*, 144.

22. Of course, this does not mean Clark and his men abjured vengeance or racial hatred.

23. "George Rogers Clark to George Mason, November 19, 1779," James, ed., *George Rogers Clark Papers, 1771-1781*, 144–45.

24. Barnhart, *Henry Hamilton and George Rogers Clark in the American Revolution*, 182–83; "Clark's Memoir," James, ed., *George Rogers Clark Papers, 1771–1781*, 288; "Major Bowman's Journal," in Pirtle, ed., *Col. George Rogers Clark's Sketch of his Campaign in the Illinois in 1778–1779*, 107.

25. Barnhart, *Henry Hamilton and George Rogers Clark in the American Revolution*, 183. Hamilton's observation suggests that Clark had personally participated in the executions, whereas Clark and Bowman indicated that their soldiers did the deed. Where historians come down on the question seems to have more to do with their views of Clark than the available evidence. A third version posits that a man in Captain Richard Montgomery's company sought the role to avenge members of his family who had been killed during Indian raids. Bakeless, *Background to Glory*, 202. Richard White, in his brilliant examination of conflict in the Great Lakes Region, examines how the telling of these executions played into various themes that served different interests, attitudes, and perceptions which are beyond the scope of this study. White, *The Middle Ground*, 375–78.

26. Barnhart, *Henry Hamilton and George Rogers Clark in the American Revolution*, 183–84.

27. "Clark's Memoir," James, ed., *George Rogers Clark Papers, 1771–1781*, 286.

28. Barnhart, *Henry Hamilton and George Rogers Clark in the American Revolution*, 184.

29. "Clark's Memoir," James, ed., *George Rogers Clark Papers, 1771–1781*, 287.

30. "Major Bowman's Journal," in Pirtle, ed., *Col. George Rogers Clark's Sketch of his Campaign in the Illinois in 1778–1779*, 107–8. Hamilton had a slightly different interpretation, but the gist was the same.

31. "Clark's Memoir," James, ed., *George Rogers Clark Papers, 1771–1781*, 289.

32. "Major Bowman's Journal," in Pirtle, ed., *Col. George Rogers Clark's Sketch of his Campaign in the Illinois in 1778-1779*, 108; Barnhart, ed., *Henry Hamilton and George Rogers Clark in the American Revolution*, 186.

33. Barnhart, *Henry Hamilton and George Rogers Clark in the American Revolution*, 187–88.

34. "Clark's Memoir," James, ed., *George Rogers Clark Papers, 1771–1781*, 290–91; "Major Bowman's Journal," in Pirtle, ed., *Col. George Rogers Clark's Sketch of his Campaign in the Illinois in 1778–1779*, 109.

EPILOGUE

1. Eric Sterner, *Anatomy of a Massacre: The Destruction of Gnadenhutten, 1782* (Yardley, PA: Westholme Publishing, 2020), 99.

2. Harrison, *George Rogers Clark and the War in the West*, 66.

3. Ibid., 67. Although serious, Bowman's burns from the burst cannon were not incapacitating and the newly promoted major continued moving about the Illinois Country in the spring and summer of 1779. His death appears to have come as a surprise. John Wayland, *The Bowmans: A Pioneering Family in Virginia, Kentucky, and the Northwest Territory* (Staunton, VA: The McClure Company, Inc., 1943), 96–98.

4. Harrison, *George Rogers Clark and the War in the West*, 71.

5. Phill Greenwalt, "Battle of Fort San Carlos—Westernmost Battle of the American Revolution," Emerging Revolutionary War Era, May 31, 2019, https://emergingrevolutionary-war.org/2019/05/31/battle-of-fort-san-carlos-westernmost-battle-of-the-american-revoluti on/; "The Battle of St. Louis," https://revolutionarywar.us/year-1780/battle-st-louis/"; Harrison, *George Rogers Clark and the War in the West*, 71.

6. Russell Mahan, *The Kentucky Kidnappings and Death March: The Revolutionary War at Ruddell's Fort and Martin's Station* (West Haven, UT: Historical Enterprises, 2020).
7. Harrison, *George Rogers Clark and the War in the West*, 74–75.
8. Ibid., 81.
9. Ibid., 83.
10. Ibid., 91.
11. Ibid., chapter 6. Clark prepared an early draft of his memoirs in the form of a long letter intended to serve as the foundation for a book, but it was not completed in his lifetime. I have referred to this letter as his memoirs, rather than the version edited and published later.
12. Pekka Hamalainen, *Indigenous Continent: The Epic Contest for North America* (New York: Liveright, 2022), 314. Hamalainen, for example, calls out the execution of Indians outside Fort Sackville without mentioning the Indians were part of a war party conveying prisoners and scalps to what they thought was a friendly location, meaning they were returning from a successful raid involving kidnapping and murder.

Bibliography

Alvord, Clarence Walworth, ed. *Cahokia Records 1778–1790*, Collections of the Illinois State Historical Library, Volume II, Virginia Series, Vol. I. Springfield: Illinois State Historical Library, 1907.

Bakeless, John. *Background to Glory: The Life of George Rogers Clark*. Lincoln: University of Nebraska Press, 1957.

Barnhart, John D., ed. *Henry Hamilton and George Rogers Clark in the American Revolution with the Unpublished Journal of Lieut. Gov. Henry Hamilton*. Crawfordsville, IN: R.E. Banta, 1951.

Blackbird, Andrew J. *History of the Ottawa and Chippewa Indians of Michigan; A Grammar of Their Language, and Personal and Family History of the Author*. Ypsilanti, MI: The Ypsilantian Job Printing House, 1887.

Bodley, Temple. *George Rogers Clark: His Life and Public Services*. Boston, MA: Houghton Mifflin Company, 1926.

Butler, Mann. *A History of the Commonwealth of Kentucky*. Louisville, KY: Wilcox, Dickerman & Co., 1834.

Butterfield, Consul Wilshire. *History of George Rogers Clark's Conquest of the Illinois and the Wabash Towns 1778 and 1779*. Columbus: The Ohio State Archeological and Historical Society, 1904.

Calloway, Colin G. *The Shawnees and the War for America*. New York: Viking, 2007.

Carter, Clarence Edwin. *Great Britain and the Illinois Country, 1763–1774*. Washington, DC: The American Historical Association, 1910.

Cotterill, R. S. *History of Pioneer Kentucky*. Cincinnati, OH: Johnson & Hardin, 1917.

Crawford, Michael J., ed. *Naval Documents of the American Revolution, Volume XI, American Theater: January 1, 1778–March 31, 1778, European Theater: January 1, 1778–March 31, 1778*. Washington, DC: Naval Historical Center, 2005.

Crawford, Michael J., ed. *Naval Documents of the American Revolution, Volume XII*. Washington, DC: Naval Historical Center, 2013.

Crytzer, Brady. *War in the Peaceable Kingdom: The Kittanning Raid of 1756*. Yardley, PA: Westholme Publishing, 2016.

Dacus, Jeff. "James Willing and the Mississippi Expedition," *Journal of the American Revolution* (April 18, 2019), https://allthingsliberty.com/2019/04/james-willing-and-the-mississippi-expedition/.

Dispenza, Brother Joseph. *Forgotten Patriot: A Story of Father Pierre Gibault*. Notre Dame, IN: Dujarie Press, 1966.

Donnelly, Joseph P. *Pierre Gibault, Missionary 1737–1802*. Chicago: Loyola University Press, 1971.

Drury, Bob and Tom Clavin. *Blood and Treasure: Daniel Boone and the Fight for America's First Frontier*. New York: St. Martin's Press, 2021.

Duckworth, Major Eric J. "Great Things Have Been Done by a Few Men: Operational Art in Clark's Illinois Campaign of 1778–1779." Fort Leavenworth, KS: School of Advanced Military Studies, United States Army Command and General Staff College, 2011.

English, William Hayden. *Conquest of the Country Northwest of the Ohio River 1778–1783 and Life of Gen. George Rogers Clark* in 2 volumes. Indianapolis, IN: The Bowen-Merrill Company, 1897.

Fitzpatrick, Alan. *In their Own Words: Native American Voices from the American Revolution*. Benwood, WV: Fort Henry Publications, 2009.

Fitzpatrick, Alan. *Wilderness War on the Ohio, New Revised Second Edition*. Benwood, WV: Fort Henry Publications, 2003.

Greenwalt, Phill. "Battle of Fort San Carlos—Westernmost Battle of the American Revolution." Emerging Revolutionary War Era, May 31, 2019, https://emergingrevolutionarywar.org/2019/05/31/battle-of-fort-san-carlos-westernmost-battle-of-the-american-revolution/.

Hamalainen, Pekka. *Indigenous Continent: The Epic Contest for North America*. New York: Liveright, 2022.

Hammon, Neal O. and Richard Taylor. *Virginia's Western War, 1775–1786*. Mechanicsburg, PA: Stackpole Books, 2002.

Harrison, Lowell H. *George Rogers Clark and the War in the West*, Kindle ed. Lexington: University Press of Kentucky, 1976.

Hellier, Cathy. "Out of Adversity: The Smallpox Census," Colonial Williamsburg, May 1, 2020, https://www.colonialwilliamsburg.org/learn/deep-dives/out-adversity-smallpox-census/.

Hutchins, Thomas. *A Topographical Description of Virginia, Pennsylvania, Maryland, and North Carolina*. London: Thomas Hutchins, 1778.

James, James Alton, ed. *George Rogers Clark Papers, 1771–1781*, Collections of the Illinois State Historical Library, Volume VIII, Virginia Series, Volume III. Springfield: Illinois State Historical Society, 1912.

Kling, Stephen, Jr., ed. *The American Revolutionary War in the West*. St. Louis, MO: THGC Publishing, 2020.

Law, Judge. *The Colonial History of Vincennes under the French, British and American Governments*. Vincennes, IN: Harvey, Mason & Co., 1858.

Lee, Jacob F. *Masters of the Middle Waters: Indian Nations and Colonial Ambitions along the Mississippi*. Cambridge, MA: Harvard University Press, 2019.

MacLeod, Normand. *Detroit to Fort Sackville, 1778–1779: The Journal of Normand MacLeod*. Detroit, MI: Wayne State University Press, 1978.

Mahan, Russell. *The Kentucky Kidnappings and Death March: The Revolutionary War at Ruddell's Fort and Martin's Station*. West Haven, UT: Historical Enterprises, 2020.

Martin, James Kirby and David L. Preston, eds. *Theaters of the American Revolution*. Yardley, PA: Westholme Publishing, 2017.

Mason, Edward G., ed. *Early Chicago and Illinois*, Chicago Historical Society, Vol. IV. Chicago: Fergus Printing Company, 1890.

Mason, Edward G., ed. *Philippe De Rocheblave and Rocheblave Papers*, Fergus Historical Series, No. 34. Chicago: Fergus Printing Company, 1890.

McDonnell, Michael A. *Masters of Empire: Great Lakes Indians and the Making of America*, Kindle ed. New York: Hill and Wang, 2015.

McMillen, Christian. "*UVA and the History of Race: The George Rogers Clark Statute and Native Americans*," UVAToday, July 27, 2020, https://news.virginia.edu/content/uva-and-history-race-george-rogers-clark-statue-and-native-americans.

Morgan, M. J. *Land of Big Rivers: French & Indian Illinois 1699–1778*. Carbondale: Southern Illinois University Press, 2010.

Morrissey, Robert Michael. *Empire by Collaboration: Indians, Colonists, and Governments in Colonial Illinois Country*. Philadelphia: University of Pennsylvania-Press, 2015.

Nester, William H. *George Roger Clark: "I Glory in War."* Norman: University of Oklahoma Press, 2012.

O'Malley, Nancy. *Boonesborough Unearthed: Frontier Archeology at a Revolutionary Fort*. Lexington: University Press of Kentucky, 2019.

O'Shaughnessy, Andrew Jackson. *The Men Who Lost America: British Leadership, the American Revolution, and the Fate of the Empire*. New Haven, CT: Yale University Press, 2013.

Palmer, Frederick. *Clark of the Ohio: A Life of George Rogers Clark*. New York: Dodd, Mead & Company, 1929.

Pirtle, Henry, ed. *Col. George Rogers Clark's Sketch of the Campaign in Illinois in 1778–1779*. Cincinnati, OH: Robert Clarke & Co., 1869.

Pittman, Captain Philip. *The Present State of the European Settlements on the Mississippi*. London: J. Nourse, 1770.

Potter, William L. *Redcoats on the Frontier: A Study of the King's 8th Regiment in North America*. Self-published, 2023.

Potts, Gwynne Tuell. *George Rogers Clark and William Croghan*. Lexington: University Press of Kentucky, 2020.

Rappleye, Charles. *Robert Morris: Financier of the American Revolution*. New York: Simon & Schuster, 2010.

Report of the Pioneer and Historical Society of the State of Michigan, Vol. IX. Lansing, MI: Thorp & Godfrey, State Printers and Binders, 1886.

Roosevelt, Theodore. *The Winning of the West*. New York: G.P. Putnam's Sons, 1889.

Roselli, Bruno. *Vigo: A Forgotten Builder of the American Republic*. Boston, MA: The Stratford Company, 1933.

Seineke, Kathrine Wagner. *The George Rogers Clark Adventure in the Illinois*. New Orleans, LA: Polyanthos, 1981.

Selby, John E. *The Revolution in Virginia, 1775–1783*. Williamsburg, VA: The Colonial Williamsburg Foundation, 1988.

Smith, Charles R. *Marines in the Revolution: A History of the Continental Marines in the American Revolution, 1775–1783*. Washington, DC: History and Museums Division, United States Marine Corps, 1975.

Starkey, Dan B. *George Rogers Clark and His Illinois Campaign*. Milwaukee, WI: Parkman Club Publications No. 12, 1897.

Sterner, Eric. "Chief Cornstalk's American Revolution, part one," *Emerging Revolutionary War Era*, April 18, 2018, https://emergingrevolutionarywar.org/2018/04/18/155233/.

Sterner, Eric. "Chief Cornstalk's American Revolution (part two)," *Emerging Revolutionary War Era*, April 25, 2018, https://emergingrevolutionarywar.org/2018/04/25/chief-cornstalks-american-revolution-part-two/.

Suchak, Sanjay. "Photos: Removal of the George Rogers Clark Statue," *UVAToday*, July 21, 2021, https://news.virginia.edu/content/photos-removal-george-rogers-clark-statue.

Thwaites, Rueben Gold and Louise Phelps Kellogg, eds. *Frontier Defense on the Upper Ohio, 1777–1778*, Draper Series, Volume III. Madison: Wisconsin Historical Society, 1912.

Waller, George M. *The American Revolution in the West.* Chicago, IL: Nelson-Hall, 1976.

Wayland, John. *The Bowmans: A Pioneering Family in Virginia, Kentucky, and the Northwest Territory.* Staunton, VA: The McClure Company, Inc., 1943.

Weddle, Kevin J. *The Compleat Victory: Saratoga and The American Revolution.* New York: Oxford University Press, 2021.

White, Richard. *The Middle Ground: Indians, Empires, and Republics in the Great Lakes Region, 1650–1814, 20th Anniversary Edition.* New York: Cambridge University Press, 2011.

Williams, Glenn F. *Dunmore's War: The Last Conflict of America's Colonial Era.* Yardley, PA: Westholme Publishing, 2017.

Acknowledgments

*R*esearching and writing can be rather solitary experiences, but producing a book most decidedly is not. A lot of folks made this survey of the Illinois campaign possible. Without them, it would not exist. At Westholme Publishing, Bruce H. Franklin has supported my exploration of the American Revolution on the frontier since my first book, *Anatomy of a Massacre: The Destruction of Gnadenhutten, 1782* and its sequel, *The Battle of Upper Sandusky, 1782*. He must be the hardest working man in publishing and the main reason Westholme has become a leading publisher of history titles. Christine Florie did a great job editing and corralling some of my odd syntax. Trudi Gershenov produced a beautiful cover and Paul Rossman created a really nice theater map. Thanks to everybody.

Don N. Hagist opened the door for me to write about the American Revolution in the *Journal of the American Revolution* and published some of my earliest studies of the war on the frontier. Rob Orrison and Phill Greenwalt, co-founders of the *Emerging Revolutionary War Era*, gave me a second writing home where I explored various aspects of the war in the West, and encouraged the project over the last few years. I first tackled Clark's Illinois campaign and James Willing's expedition for them. Dan Welch reviewed an early draft of the manuscript and shared his own talents as a writer and editor. Gabe Neville reviewed a draft of the book and shared his excellent editing skills, not to mention his own ample knowledge of the

Revolutionary War on the frontier and familiarity with source material I hadn't found on my own. Thanks, gents.

Till the Extinction of This Rebellion was several years in the making, governed largely by the challenges of visiting the places Clark and his men traveled. COVID cancelled my first trip when everything closed in 2020. Circumstances conspired in 2021 to force another postponement. But, in 2022 my brother Dave Sterner and I finally made it out to the frontier to visit some of the most important sites. Thanks, Dave, for the company, some photos, and indulging me when I geeked out with local historians. I also have to thank my nephew, Brad Sterner, for heading out to take some photos on short notice. Tim Harwarth gave the manuscript a last minute read and sanity check. Thanks to everyone.

At Vincennes, Dave and I met with Joe Herron and Frank Doughman of the National Park Service at George Rogers Clark National Historical Park. Joe kindly gave us a preview of an annual winter hike along Clark's most likely route from the Wabash to Vincennes and explained the different attempts to nail that route down using the limited data available from participants, modern topographical studies, data drawn from advanced geographic information systems models, and good old-fashioned shoe leather. Additionally, Joe, Frank, and their colleague James Mattoon graciously shared their knowledge and work with us while I tried to make sense of contradictory accounts of the Battle of Fort Sackville from Clark, Bowman, and Hamilton. They've undoubtedly forgotten more about Clark than I will ever know and helped me work through some of my early misconceptions. All the remaining errors are mine. It is impossible to say enough good things about the National Park Service, its allies, and the important work they do in preserving, protecting, researching, and interpreting the large number of parks set aside all over the country, whether they are built around nature or history. In so many ways, they make sure that our parks remain a national treasure available to everyone. So, I owe them my thanks not only for guidance, but also their public service.

With that in mind, I'd be remiss if I failed to thank the unnamed staff at various state, regional, county, and local parks in Ohio, Indiana, and Kentucky: Fort Defiance, Pontiac Park, and Grand Rapids Park in Ohio, the Forks of the Wabash, Prophetstown, nearby Tippecanoe battlefield, Fort Ouiatenon, and the Falls of the Ohio State Park in Indiana, and multiple parks in Kentucky, including the Isaac Shelby Cemetery, Harrodsburg, Fort Boonesborough, Blue Licks Battlefield, and Limestone Landing. Whether they're living historians, park guides, volunteers, management, or maintenance staff, the work of these folks is crucial in maintaining our ability to see, hear, and experience much of America's history. Like the National Park Service, they're often under-resourced and under-staffed, but still accomplish incredible things with what they have. We all owe the people committed to protecting these sites, whether federal, state, regional, county, local, or private, along with their defenders and advocates, a debt of gratitude.

Index